WHOLENESS AND HOLINESS IN EDUCATION
AN ISLAMIC PERSPECTIVE

To the source of my inspiration

To the twin souls of my parents, whose unwavering devotion to God,
love for their children and humankind, wisdom, generosity,
purity & gentleness planted & nurtured the wholeness
and holiness of my religion in me. They allowed me to
grow freely in search of the truth of the temporary
world, & their absence has inspired me to
search for the truth of eternal life.
This work is dedicated to their
souls with my love
& gratitude.

WHOLENESS
and
HOLINESS
in
EDUCATION

An Islamic Perspective

ZAHRA AL ZEERA

THE INTERNATIONAL INSTITUTE OF ISLAMIC THOUGHT

THE INTERNATIONAL INSTITUTE OF ISLAMIC THOUGHT
P.O. BOX 669, HERNDON, VA 22070, USA

LONDON OFFICE
P.O. BOX 126, RICHMOND, SURREY TW9 2UD, UK

ISBN 1-56564-280-5 paperback
ISBN 1-56564-279-1 hardback

Cover design and typesetting by Sohail Nakhooda
Printed in the United Kingdom
by Biddles Limited, Guildford and King's Lynn

ACKNOWLEDGEMENTS

AUTHOR

I wish to express my heartfelt gratitude to the International Institute of Islamic Thought, especially Dr. Fathi Malkawi, its Executive Director, who encouraged the idea of publishing this book, and Dr. Anas al Shaikh Ali, Academic Advisor of the London Office, who undertook the painstaking responsibility of preparing the manuscript for publication. I also extend my appreciation to all those who participated in reviewing the manuscript and providing insightful comments and feedback, including Dr. Louay Safi, Ebrahim Kalim and H. White. Finally, I thank my family and friends Dr. Dolores Furlong, Dr. Dana Sheik, Dr. Asad Sheik, Adam Sheik, and Haya Abdulla for their unflagging support, in the ups and downs of writing this book.

PUBLISHER

The IIIT wishes to thank the editorial and production team at the London Office and those who were directly or indirectly involved in the completion of this book: Ataiya Pathan, Sylvia Hunt, Sohail Nakhooda and Shiraz Khan. We would also like to express our thanks and gratitude to Dr. Zahra Al Zeera, who, throughout the various stages of the book's production, helped by responding to our various queries and suggestions.

CONTENTS

FOREWORD

In his Introduction to Malik Badri's *Contemplation: An Islamic Psychospiritual Study,* recently published by IIIT, Shaykh Yūsuf al-Qaraḍāwī highlighted the problem of the dependency of the Muslim world on the West in all branches of modern knowledge and urged Muslim specialists to "take an independent line" and to "adopt an attitude of inquiry and criticism instead of passive acceptance," especially in the human and social sciences, which by their very nature can never be as "neutral" or value-free as the "pure," "hard," natural sciences.

This is not the place to explore in any depth the vexed question as to how truly neutral or value-free even "pure" science really is, especially in its unremittingly reductionist mode of blinkered scientism, but it will suffice to say that it takes little intelligence and reflection to perceive that the apparatus of dogmatic scientism, though claiming to operate under the most rigorous conditions of objectivity, is nevertheless founded on a priori assumptions germane to the Western secular world-view of positivism which radically restricts the nature of reality only to that which is observable and measurable by quantitative means.

Implicit in this conceptual paradigm is, indeed, not only a set of crippling perceptual handicaps but also a set of culturally determined *values* whose logical consequence is the *devaluation* of man and the cosmos through the denial of God and of any unseen dimension or divine purpose in the creation of the universe. From an Islamic perspective, the denial of God does not elevate man, for it is of course the underlying unity and interconnectedness of everything in existence which makes the microcosm of man a mirror of the macrocosm and which alone endows man with the possibility of becoming fully human by virtue of his divinely appointed role as *khalīfah*, or vicegerent.

This treatise, *Wholeness and Holiness in Education*, by Dr. Zahra Al Zeera, is a further contribution to the vital work of the 'Islamization of knowledge,' of which Dr. Badri's work is an outstanding example in the field of psychology. Indeed, she continues the tradition of reviving a truly holistic perspective, paradigm or world-view founded on *tawḥīd*, the affirmation of God's Oneness, the ruling idea in Islam.

I say "reviving" this perspective, because the open-mindedness and multi-dimensionality of thought encouraged by a vision of the unity of all knowledge are part of the rich intellectual heritage of Islam. Authentic 'Islamization of knowledge' cannot be a parochial concern but must be an inclusive activity which avoids the limitation and fixity of a mono-perspective by acknowledging and valuing different levels of description, by synthesizing and integrating traditional and contemporary knowledge, or perennial and acquired knowledge, by going beyond facile dichotomies representing competing models of reality, and by reconciling opposites and resolving contradictions within an over-arching Islamic paradigm. This unity, after all, is by definition what the doctrine of *tawḥīd* implies in the domain of knowledge.

But of course it does not mean that the Islamic perspective is conducive to the "anything goes" relativism of a constructivist paradigm which fails to acknowledge any absolute or objective reality. As the author herself demonstrates in her discussion of phenomenology as a valid research method within the Islamic paradigm, Abū al Rayhān al-Bīrūnī, in his classical study of the religion and culture of India, was using sophisticated "constructivist" methods of inquiry a thousand years ago, including interviews through which Hindus spoke for themselves to reveal their own "stories" and construct their own realities; participant observation; analysis of documents in the original language, and comparison of Hindu thought with Greek, Sufi and Christian concepts so as to attempt to discover the human thread connecting all ancient cultures. Let it not be forgotten either that al-Bīrūnī was also seeking to gain new knowledge from Hindu culture in the same way as Greek thought was absorbed and utilised by other Muslim scholars.

However, as the author points out, what makes such a study crucially distinct from a merely relativist study is not the methodology - for this triangulation of methods is as compatible with the Islamic paradigm as it is with the constructivist approach - it is rather the framework within which the multiplicity of knowledge is interpreted. The power of Islamic science is that it conceives of knowledge not *horizontally* (which, as Seyyed Hossein Nasr has observed, results in knowledge of God and the angels being ranked on the same level as knowledge of molluscs), but *hierarchically*, making possible the realization that multiplicity is only the manifestation of a single reality, the ultimate truth.

Through this paradigm we can grasp the underlying unity of science and religion, physics and metaphysics, knowledge and values, and all other domains of knowledge and activity which have often been pitted against each other as a battery of irreconcilable dichotomies - the human and the divine, the phenomenal and the metaphenomenal, the mutable and the eternal, the material and the sacred, the personal and the social, the rational and the intuitive, the exoteric and the esoteric, the theoretical and the practical, the idealistic and the realistic, the active and the passive, and so on.

Dr. Al Zeera identifies "dialectical thinking" as the means of transcending the limitations of dichotomization. This advanced style of thought places the human being in an "interworld," an isthmus, meeting-place or *barzakh*, at the intersection of interaction. It strives to unify opposites, affirming and incorporating logical polarities rather than seeking to avoid contradiction and paradox through one-sided adherence to a single perspective. Of great importance is her conclusion that dialectical thinking (and the intellectual connectedness which its promotes) should be one of the major planks of a holistic education, together with reflection and meditation (which enable learners to connect with their inner selves and therefore promote spiritual connectedness) and conversation and dialogue (which enable individuals to connect with others and the society in which they live).

Significantly, the author refers to the work of Riegel, who identifies the ability to accept contradictions, constructive confrontations and asynchronies as the highest stage of cognitive development, and to the work of Fowler, who associates dialectical thinking with the development of faith. It goes without saying that the dialectical process is not one either of compromise or loose relativism, but one of creative tension which ultimately transforms contradictions into complementarities, releasing the open-minded thinker from ingrained habits and conditioned patterns of thought, established affiliations, fear of change and instability, and reluctance to approach anything which may be threatening to one's sense of "self."

The connection Dr. Al Zeera makes between this transformative state and the theory of dissipative structures developed by the Nobel-prize winning physical chemist, Ilya Prigogine, is instructive, for, according to Prigogine, physical systems have the capacity to go through periods of instability and then self-organization, resulting in more complex systems. Thus, "instability," in its positive sense of freedom from one-sided, crystallized thinking, is the key to greater coherence and complexity. On a more mystical level, the ultimate "resting place" of the one who has attained to God-consciousness (taqwa), the station of permanent "abiding" in God, is paradoxically a state of total openness and surrender, a place of "no-place" in which the limited self is extinguished. This can be equated with the sixth and final stage of Fowler's map of faith development, the stage attained only through grace, in which there is a complete sacrifice of stability.

It is this unitive vision of knowledge which is at the heart of Dr. Al Zeera's treatise. By showing that the dominant positivist paradigm, with its insistence on dispassionate "objectivity," and the alternative constructivist or interpretive paradigm with its subjective, multiple realities, are in fact both limited to the mundane level and equally in denial of any transcendent reality, she clears the way for the systematic exposition of a truly holistic Islamic paradigm and the "transformative" research tools and educational methods which it generates. While we have to wait until well into the second half of the treatise for the unveiling of methods for holistic education, this reflects the broader conceptual purpose and carefully constructed design of the treatise, which, thesis-like, painstakingly builds up the case upon which its holistic educational applications are founded.

It would be mistaken, however, to conclude that the author's critique of existing paradigms and her espousal of a super-ordinate Islamic paradigm are intellectual exercises divorced from her personal experience, for it is one of her axioms that the mind and the soul of the researcher or scholar should not be artificially separated in the interest of a spurious "objectivity" or "professionalism". Moving away from the positivist paradigm and its fragmentation of the oneness of our experience demands, in her words, that we "follow the golden thread of [our] own spiritual experience" (without this ever becoming a narcissistic preoccupation divorced from society), and she enacts her own belief in the validity and importance of personal experiences and narrative inquiry as research tools by candidly charting her own spiritual and intellectual journey. In so doing she shows how her discovery and espousal of the reconciling power of "dialectical thinking" was not simply the outcome of an "objective" research design but the resolution of a major personal conflict between the demands of the narrowly focused intellectual activity expected of a researcher and her own spiritual aspiration and need for wholeness which could not be encompassed by the limited paradigms on offer.

The thrust of the author's critique of positivism is in accordance with Dr. Badri's own refutation of reductionist approaches to psychology which would strip human beings of any conscious feelings or intentions, complex cognitive processes, soul or spiritual essence, and equate the thinking mind simply with the mechanisms of brain chemistry.

Such a critique is unsurprising from anyone, Muslim or non-Muslim, with the ability to reflect on the "signs within themselves" and in the created world. Of particular interest and significance, however, is her realization of the limitations of constructivism, despite its scope for naturalistic and humanistic methods of inquiry which have the *appearance* of a holistic approach because they recognise the validity of subjective human experiences. Although this approach is certainly less fragmented than a positivist outlook, and can therefore serve, as she says, as a "back door into spirituality," it is still unremittingly "this-relative and this-worldly" and fragments reality into the multiple, contextualized realities of "what is seen, felt and perceived by people" without any reference to a "given," transcendent, comprehensive, all-encompassing, unifying reality. Similarly, the "single reality" of positivism is most certainly not the One Reality of *tawḥīd*, even though it is driven by the "objective" search for immutable laws and mechanisms.

Education is a field which is particularly vulnerable to changing ideologies, but it is far too important to be a battleground between competing paradigms. Many "visionary" educators in the secular West are now advocating a radical paradigm shift away from what they consider to be an obsolete machine-age "performance" model of education with its emphasis on teacher-centered transmission of content through rigidly specified objectives and prescribed outcomes, and the accompanying over-emphasis on the acquisition of analytical reasoning skills. They favour a systemic model which demands synthetic, interactive thinking and creative problem-solving skills able to yield understanding and explanation rather than mere accumulation of information - a learner-centered culture promoting self-directed and lifelong learning skills, social responsibility and ethical values.

These competing models in many ways mirror the fundamental dichotomy between positivist and constructivist worldviews explored in this treatise, and just as the author exposes the limitations of both of them, so we must always bear in mind that whatever models govern the development of secular curricula, even those models which appear to be moving towards a holistic vision, these programs are limited human constructions wholly concerned with the horizontal dimension of education and cannot be the basis for a truly holistic Islamic curriculum in which the vertical dimension is the primary axis of development. The horizontal and vertical dimensions are the "temporal" and "perennial" domains of knowledge recognised by both Ibn Sina and al-Ghazālī in their theories of knowledge, and it is of course perennial knowledge which the Muslim strives to attain and which temporal knowledge in all its forms merely serves.

Only a curriculum in harmony with the teachings of the Holy Qur'an and intended to integrate man's understanding of God, the universe and his own nature can be spacious enough to accommodate and reconcile competing paradigms. The Islamic perspective, always seeking unity, harmony and balance, does not conceive, for example, of analytic and synthetic modes of thought as conflicting styles, the former to be superseded by the latter in the revolutionary school of tomorrow, but as complementary capacities, each with its appropriate domain. If the left side of the brain is overused, the corrective is not to go overboard for "right-brained" thinking but to seek a balance between the two sides. Similarly, we need not become disillusioned with *science* because of the myopic vision of *scientism*. The author refers to the important statement of al-Ghazālī that laborious study of the sciences dealing with fact and demonstration is indispensable if the soul is to avoid imaginative delusions masquerading as spiritual enlightenment.

This is not to say that major correctives are not sometimes required, and in many respects Dr. Al Zeera is surely right in appealing for the recognition and valuation of feminine intuition and spirituality in a world dominated by masculine rationality, although we must be careful not to fall into the trap of equating the masculine and the feminine entirely with the male and female gender, for they have far greater explanatory power as complementary principles, as *yang* and *yin*, within the individual. In a very real sense, the fundamental dichotomies explored in this treatise can be subsumed under the vast subject of gender relations, a subject which needs urgent discussion in the Muslim world.

The vision of unity conveyed by the author is all the more impressive for the sincerity and sense of deep personal engagement she brings to bear upon material which has clearly played a major part in her own personal transformation. The challenge now is for Muslim educationalists to pursue the detailed implications of the broad educational principles and methods she derives from the holistic Islamic paradigm.

Shawwal 1421   DR. JEREMY HENZELL-THOMAS
January 2001   *The Association of Muslim Social Scientists (UK)*
                      The Book Foundation (UK)

AUTHOR'S INTRODUCTION

To write about Islamic epistemology, the Islamic paradigm and Islamic education is an almost impossible task. The journey through this book for me was like trying to cross the ocean in a small boat with very few skills and little knowledge of sailing. On setting out, one is mesmerized by the beauty and majesty of the ocean, the gigantic waves breaking aggressively on the shores, and the gentle breeze touching the soul and creating a mysterious feeling of love and ecstasy. At that point, we seekers and followers of the path are torn between what we see as a potential for learning while unveiling the mystery of theology, philosophy, and mysticism and making it accessible to myself, my students, and all seekers of knowledge. I was, however, well aware of my limitations and the overwhelming scope of Islamic knowledge. But when I was driven to the ocean of Islamic knowledge by some unknown force, a quiet inner voice and an aggressive intellectual passion that demanded to know, I did not have much choice. The decision to write this book was extremely challenging, but the seeds were planted in 1989 in my doctoral thesis, when I was ten years younger and more open to challenges and risks. I had to go through the ebb and flow of the dialectic of the adventurous spirit of risk-taking and the wisdom of years. The result was this book.

I sailed: with me were the excitement of venturing on a challenging journey, an intellectual passion, a little knowledge, and an unwavering faith in God that He would lead me to the right path to see a glimpse of the Truth. My compass on those rough seas and during the stormy nights was my unquestionable trust in God. My intention was to seek knowledge and share it with others, as we teachers are obligated to do according to the Sacred Book of Islam. So I comforted myself and said that if I was doing my duty and following an inner voice as well, God was certainly going to guide me.

Besides trust, faith, and hard work, thinking dialectically kept the balance between demands of the mind and those of the soul. Dialectical thinking is the backbone of this book. So it will be explained in detail in Chapter 9 owing to its importance as a way of thinking to understand wholeness in life and, God willing, produce holistic knowledge. The reader, therefore, is advised to read the section on dialectical thinking with an open and fresh mind, leaving aside preconceived notions of the dialectics and its association with Marx's dialectical realism and Hegel's dialectical idealism. The concept of dialectics is used in this context because the word 'dialectics' has the ability to encompass opposing ideas so as to integrate and create a synthesis and an original idea. Without dialectical thinking, I believe, one could hardly make sense of the contradictions embedded in wholeness. Islamic sciences are so diverse, vast, and complex that opening one door leads to other doors and one can easily feel – happily though – that she or he is lost from the very beginning. It is the wholeness and the unique characteristics of Islamic knowledge that intermingle and interrelate all knowledge. There are no barriers between different fields. All start with the name of God and all end with the name of God. All aim at realizing the Truth by understanding the microcosm and the macrocosm. Realization of the Absolute Truth is at the center and the core, no matter what the subject or the field – natural and physical sciences, social sciences, cosmology, or geography – and that is what makes Islamic science unique. The method of dialectical thinking is important because it leads to a realization of oneness and unity in the universe and the self. The dialogue or the conflict between contradictory ideas leads eventually to one original idea that is the synthesis of the opposing ideas.

The chapters that follow seek to present certain aspects of Islamic epistemology from an *educational point of view* rather than a philosophical or theoretical perspective. The emphasis, however, is on methods used for the production of knowledge that are suitable for Islamic societies and Islamic culture. The choice of research methods and strategies becomes a question relating to the issue of what counts as valid social science, to be answered with reference to the criteria of what counts as valid scientific knowledge. Are all research methods and their related paradigms equally valid? Do they all have a role to play in social and personal research? How are we to understand the relations between them? Questions such as these are of major concern in this book. Transformation through research methods and learning strategies are therefore also major concerns in the following chapters.

In addition to issues related to knowledge production, this book is concerned with methods of knowledge acquisition and transformation from teaching and learning. Wholeness, unity, harmony, and balance are important concepts not only in the development of Islamic programs and educational systems, but also in all situations, from the microcosm to the macrocosm, from the self to the universe. Polarization and contradictions are inherent in all life. Negative and positive forces interrelate continually to maintain living beings and to contribute to their evolution, growth, and development. Awareness of the principles of wholeness, unity, multiplicity, and the relationship between them helps one develop understanding, openness, tolerance, and integrity. This awareness helps people to operate on a wider base of knowledge by which they can see above and beyond the information provided by the senses. It also helps individuals to experience and realize unity through the very multiplicity of the self, nature, and the universe. In this way, individuals can learn that God created contradictions not to be fought against, but as the means to discover and understand the subtle intelligence of the One and the many at various levels and different dimensions. People can then realize the forces of growth and evolution and work with these forces instead of against them.

Part I comprises two chapters. The first chapter deals with personal experiences and includes a brief reference to my intellectual and spiritual journey. The second chapter presents spirituality from a woman's perspective. It is this part that contributes, I hope, to the paradigm shift in contemporary Islamic literature. By that, I mean the inclusion of personal experiences as the base for discovering and revealing stories or events in the past and the way in which those events have participated in knowledge acquisition and knowledge reconstruction. Reflection on personal experiences allows one to realize the hidden meanings of events which otherwise go unnoticed. By reflecting, we are able to reconstruct our experiences in the light of the current situation and the new knowledge that we have acquired. Starting with ourselves, I

believe, is crucial for both students and scholars. If the aim is to contribute to the creation of Islamic knowledge, as most contemporary
Muslim scholars advocate, then an examination of the inner soul is
essential. In personal experiences are hidden stories of the soul, stories
that touch the core; we know that they are not only important but
sacred too. We treasure those experiences because we know they are
real, and only we know that. 'Islamic knowledge' is used in this book to
mean knowledge that is based on an Islamic paradigm and emerges
from Islamic epistemology and Islamic methodology. So both graduate
students and scholars are able to create and produce knowledge that is
appropriate for Islamic communities and addresses their concerns and
problems. Production of Islamic knowledge is a major issue in this
book; reflection on personal experience provides researchers with an
immediate, real, and original course of knowledge which has been neglected and downplayed by positivists for so long.

This book is rooted in my personal experiences. I trusted theories
of personal experiences from Plato to Dewey and trusted the wisdom
of my professor, M. Connelly, who encouraged me to tell my stories, as
he likes to refer to personal experiences, and to reflect on them. I started the journey reluctantly, believing this undertaking to be personal
and not academic nor professional. I felt uncomfortable at first, stum-
bling in the darkness of the subconscious. Gradually, I began to see a
glimmer of light here and there. Then suddenly I was on an open plain
with a blue sky flooded with sunshine. In a moment of realization, I
saw the tapestry of my life in front of me. I saw the golden thread of
spirituality and love woven in that tapestry from one end to the other. I
realized the conflict between the intellectual and spiritual sides of my
being, and I perceived the conflict between the East and West inside me
and in my society. After struggling through the conflict, I reached a
stage of reconciliation in myself and hoped that it would happen in society too. From dialogue, conversation with the 'other,' we can reach a
peaceful stage of reconciliation.

This book is the outcome of a tedious search, hard work, and reflection that started in 1989. Without such reflection, I should have continued my positivist thinking; and advanced in measurement, evaluation, and statistics. Yet, feeling empty inside and alien to myself and

my culture, I started reading Islamic classics and encyclopedic works of great Muslim scholars in 1989 after the realization of spirituality in my life, or what I call the golden thread. Ever since, I have been writing on the notions of the Islamic paradigm and tried to interweave it into my teaching and my theories of learning and teaching. Education became more meaningful to me and my students at the University when it was pursued from an Islamic, holistic perspective. On being introduced to the Islamic paradigm and Islamic epistemology in courses on evaluation and research methods, my students began analyzing and understanding theories of psychology, sociology, and education from that perspective. Their exposure to Islamic epistemology affected their entire university life. They were set on journeys of self-exploration and reflection.

Although part I of this book might seem rather unusual or even unacceptable to some scholars belonging to conventional schools of thought, because of the inclusion of my personal experiences in a scholarly work, to me it is this part that contributes to the advancement of an alternative paradigm that is a major theme of this book. One way of regaining our wholeness and holiness in education is by connecting to our inner selves through our intimate experiences. Retelling those experiences, however, allows us to reconstruct them and evaluate them in a different light. Reconstruction of experiences, I believe, facilitates transformation that should be the aim of education. Therefore, the readers of this book should remember that this is a different type of scholarly work that aims at integrating the personal and the professional, the intellectual and the spiritual, the inner and the outer so as to fulfill the thesis of wholeness and holiness in education.

My aim in writing this book is to encourage Muslim students in North America and Europe to reflect on their personal experiences, to find the golden thread in their lives, to acknowledge it and utilize it in their personal and professional lives. I want to encourage becoming whole, and acknowledging the Sacred that is inside everyone, and making it part of daily living. The moment of realizing the Sacred and acknowledging it will be a turning point in their lives, and inevitably their study will take an Islamic turn. No matter what they are studying – science, technology, sociology, psychology, or astronomy – when they start analyzing theories in those fields from an Islamic perspective, the spiritual and the sacred permeate naturally and profoundly.

Chapter 2 is a reflection on spirituality from a woman's perspective. Some readers might wonder: Why woman's spirituality in particular and not spirituality in general? The answer is simple. A quick review of what has been written on Islamic spirituality will show that men do most of the writing and that reflects the male perspective on spirituality. Being an academic woman who has a certain perspective on spirituality and on knowledge rooted in spirituality, I include this chapter to present my views and to encourage women who have different or similar views to acknowledge them and share them with others. Giving a voice to woman's spirituality as a major component of an Islamic theory of knowledge is, I believe, crucial for developing the concept of wholeness and holiness in life and education. The purpose of this chapter is to give an account of woman's spirituality in general and its effect on creating an Islamic knowledge that is whole and caters for the mind and the soul. Some readers may wonder about the relevance of spirituality to theories of knowledge. This will be discussed in detail in Chapter 2 to show the wholeness of Islamic epistemology and to explain that knowledge is both intellectual and spiritual. The core of this book is to develop an education based on Islamic epistemology that caters for both the intellectual and spiritual needs of human beings.

Islamic history is full of spiritual female luminaries that nurtured with their love and spirituality men and women who, in their turn, became great Sufi masters, scholars, and faithful believers, who defended Islam to the last drop of their blood. However, history does not focus on woman's spirituality, assuming it to be one of their natural qualities, especially the women of the *ahl al-bayt* (the family of the Prophet of Islam). In published literature, in both the East and the West, the only woman that has attracted the wide attention of scholars is Rābiʿah al-ʿAdawiyya, the mystic Sufi whose selfless love of God is known all over the world. Despite the uniqueness of Rābiʿah's mystical journey, we ordinary women, professional and non-professional, have difficulty in understanding her mysticism and her mystical journey. We live in a different time and space, yet spirituality, the golden thread, runs through the tapestry of our lives from birth to death. I am acknowledging and honoring this type of spirituality, and I call it practical spirituality: it is practiced by millions of Muslim women in the East and the West. Spirituality is woman's best-kept secret. It empowers her, enhances her, and hence provides her with different ways and means of knowing – in both knowledge acquisition and knowledge production, which are major themes in this book. Chapter 2 was inspired by three sources: Rābiʿah's mystical journey, al-Ghazālī's theory of knowledge, and the Chinese concept of *yin* and *yang*.

Part II contains two chapters. Chapter 3 is a review of literature on both the conventional and alternative paradigms, and it prepares the ground for the Islamic paradigm. For both paradigms, issues are discussed at three levels: ontological, epistemological, and methodological. The emphasis of the discussion is on the philosophical issues underpinning research methodology. Chapter 3 sheds some light on two major theoretical perspectives that have dominated the social sciences, that is, positivism and constructivism/interpretivism, the latter also called the naturalistic paradigm.

Chapter 3 is based mainly on ideas developed by Guba and Lincoln[1] on paradigms. Scientific inquirers tend to view the world, and consequently any phenomenon with which they deal, as discoverable, controllable, and fragmentable into discrete, independent atoms. By atomizing the problem, scientists investigate and control the variables under certain conditions, and manipulate specific ones so as to control some and randomize others. By doing so, constraints are imposed upon the antecedent conditions and outputs. Naturalistic inquirers make the opposite assumption of multiple realities that are interrelated and inseparable. Phenomena are considered to diverge, not to converge into a single truth as in a scientific inquiry.

Each paradigm is based on assumptions about the inquirer–participant relationship. The scientific paradigm assumes that no relationship exists between the investigator and the subject of inquiry. The inquirer believes it is possible to keep a reasonable distance from the phenomena. Constructivist/naturalistic inquirers, however, base their approach on their first assumption about interacting multiple realities, consider their own interaction among these realities, and view the interaction between researchers and subjects as extremely important.

The paradigms are founded on differing assumptions about the nature of truth. Scientific inquirers assume that the nature of reality is singular and that reality can be segmented and controlled. Consequently, inquirers force conditions for convergence and look for similarities. Obviously their concern is to generalize and develop universal rules to constitute theories, which are to be imposed on natural and social settings. Naturalistic scientists rely heavily, for collecting the data and understanding the situation, on the interaction between themselves and their participants, which is a basis for 'thick' and rich descriptions. Generalization is not usually the concern of the naturalistic inquirers because their focus is on differences, uniqueness, and idiosyncrasies, rather than on similarities. Naturalistic inquiry thus leads to the development of a specific, nonuniversal knowledge base which focuses on the understanding of particular cases.

Chapter 4 provides critical reflection on positivism and constructivism and the inappropriateness of both paradigms for the production of Islamic knowledge. All existing paradigms are fragmented and reductionist and have 'either/or' qualities. None of the paradigms, even alternative paradigms such as the naturalistic paradigm and critical theory, has the capacity for dealing with both contraries at the same time: absolute and relative, objective and subjective, fixed and temporal, and so on. My argument is based on the assumption that reality, from an Islamic point of view, is one; that reality consists of all the apparent opposites that, in fact, complement each other. Denying one side of reality, the subjective or objective, causes a split in one's consciousness and hence in our ability to perceive the whole and the one. One needs a balance between the intellectual and spiritual sides of one's being, leading to wholeness and holiness. I further explain the limitations of both paradigms with respect to encompassing metaphysical issues and concepts such as the world of the unseen, God, the Day of Judgment, and the hereafter. The Islamic paradigm is rooted in such metaphysical concepts.

Part III consists of three main chapters. Chapter 5 presents the Islamic worldview, which is religious, philosophical, and rational. It is a worldview of *tawḥīd*, of monism, regarding God as the Absolute Reality and the Source of Being. *Tawḥīd* is the essence of Islam, it is the act of affirming God to be the One, Absolute, Eternal, and Transcendent Creator.

Since *tawḥīd* is the essence of Islam, it will be discussed in detail, for the concept runs through this book as a river runs through the valleys and plains and brings life to the lands nearby. The 'dialectics of *tawḥīd*' is the basis of this book, uniting ideas and giving life to them. The concept of the 'dialectics of *tawḥīd*' – its differing and apparently opposed manifestations – might cause unease for some because of the paradoxical meaning that it carries. *Tawḥīd* means oneness and unity, whereas dialectics means opposing ideas and conflict. However, for me it is another way of understanding the 'One and the many.' Dialectics is embedded in *tawḥīd* naturally, as will be explained later: simply it is the dialectical path that leads to *tawḥīd*.

The Islamic worldview is not purely a religious one. The uniqueness of Islam is in this profound and challenging belief in both the material and the religious worlds. Muslims should live this life and enjoy God's gifts in moderation, yet believe in the hereafter and consider this life as a purposeful journey that should be cultivated from knowledge and good deeds. The knowledge and good deeds are to take them higher on the ladder of humanity and perfection, to bring them closer to God and therefore to eternal life. This blend of the two extremes is what Islam is about: a combination of religious and material life.

Chapter 6 proposes the Islamic paradigm for Islamic universities and the production of Islamic knowledge: a holistic, comprehensive, and integrated paradigm that can encompass the wholeness of Islamic thought. One of the objectives of the book is to present and establish the underlying principles of an Islamic paradigm which will lay the cornerstone for Islamic theories. The proposed Islamic paradigm includes six principles that aim at developing

1. Islamic spiritual psychology and the unity of the self;
2. Islamic epistemology and the unity of knowledge;
3. Islamic ontology and metaphysics and the unity of the cosmic order;
4. Islamic eschatology and the unity of life;
5. Islamic sociology and the unity of the community.
6. Islamic methodology of *tawḥīd* and the ultimate unity.

The common theme in all the principles of the Islamic paradigm is the dialectics of *tawḥīd*. The Islamic paradigm as a holistic, integrated paradigm is divine, spiritual, religious, eternal, constant, absolute, and ideal. On the other hand, it is human, material, rational, temporary, mutable, and relative. These two opposites are intimately interwoven by *tawḥīd*.

In brief, the Islamic paradigm is all-encompassing, developmental, purposeful, and integrated. It is based on the Qur'anic worldview and derives its principles from the Sacred Text. Thus all the principles of the Islamic paradigm lead to the realization of the unity of the divine principle. Spiritual psychology integrates body, mind, and soul as one unified whole. Because Islamic epistemology is holistic, it addresses the worldly and the scientific as well as the religious and spiritual aspects of knowledge. In addition, Islamic ontology and metaphysics address the wholeness of the cosmos and the natural order, and deal with nature and universal laws scientifically and spiritually. Moreover, Islamic eschatology deals with issues of the hereafter and the here-and-now. This draws students to think of both worlds, but to remember that this world is the means to be cultivated for the end, the hereafter. Furthermore, the Islamic methodology of *tawḥīd* helps Muslim students to understand the controversial issues of life and education. It also helps their dialectical and critical thinking, which is considered to be the highest stage of adult development. Finally, Islamic sociology deals with social and community issues, for it is considered to be the duty of every individual to participate in, develop, and improve societal life.

Part IV of the book presents transformative inquiry and consists of two chapters. After outlining the theoretical basis of the Islamic worldview – the Islamic paradigm and Islamic epistemology – this part addresses the goal of providing practical methods and strategies for university students to implement ideas presented in Part III, thus moving from theory to practice. Chapter 8, 'Transformative Research Methods,' proposes research methods of transformative inquiry. Several methods are recommended because they use open systems and dissipative structures to allow both the researcher and the phenomena under study to interact freely and grow through research. The theory of dissipative structures explains 'irreversible process' in nature: the movement toward higher and higher orders of life. It is presented in this context because it explains the mystery of transformation and its ability to offer a scientific model of transformation at every level, making it relevant to everyday life. The theory of dissipative structures is explained in detail in Chapter 8 to show its relevance to transformation and production of Islamic knowledge. However, what makes any research method Islamic is not only the method but also the Islamic paradigm used to guide the research and interpret the data.

The combination of transformative methodology and the Islamic paradigm as a means of interpreting and analyzing the data makes these methods suitable for the production of Islamic knowledge. Phenomenology, hermeneutics, heuristics, and narrative inquiry are suggested as alternative research methods that can help students and researchers in studying major sensitive issues, both holistically and meaningfully. Phenomenology and hermeneutics can be used for sociological and cultural issues, but one needs a more holistic perspective, close to the phenomena and requiring participants to reveal their stories and construct meaning from their experiences. Thus heuristic and narrative approaches lend themselves more easily to personal and intimate experiences, and so stories of the soul and the heart can be explored. The intimate relationship between the researcher and the phenomena under study transforms all parties to higher and deeper levels. More importantly, during the transformation, researchers become aware of controversial and contradictory issues and gradually realize the wholeness and oneness of the macrocosm and the microcosm.

As chapter 8 deals with methodological issues from the perspective of research and knowledge production, so chapter 9 deals with methodological issues from a teaching/learning perspective and in terms of knowledge acquisition. For a student to be able to think holistically, she or he must be trained and equipped with methods that both develop the mind and discipline the soul. Most educational institutions in the East and the West diminish human beings to the mind only, and ignore the soul. By so doing, they create unbalanced human beings that have advanced intellectual abilities, yet spiritually are poor and weak.

Methods that are suggested here are dialectical thinking, reflection and meditation, conversation, and dialogue.

The first approach is dialectical and creative thinking that will help students to develop their intellectual abilities and thus establish intellectual connectedness. Simply put, it will establish the body-mind connection. In their educational experience, some students in Islamic countries feel a spiritual vacuum that needs to be addressed properly to fulfill the mission of wholeness. Students are disconnected from their inner selves. Second, prayers, reflection, and meditation will be dealt with as worshiping rituals and therapeutic methods for connecting students with their inner selves. Spiritual connectedness can be achieved by this so that she or he becomes a whole person. It must be mentioned that no clear-cut division exists between the various human faculties. The categorization here is to clarify the ideas of connectedness, experiences, and the inner self. The third approach in the process of unifying students with their inner selves and their surroundings is to promote understanding of others by hermeneutic methods, as by conversation. In this way, communication and dialogue are established among individuals in society, between parents and children, between teachers and students, and so on. This will help students to unify the polarization in society and encourage communication. In this process, the whole person is connected with a unified society.

I

REFLECTIONS ON
PERSONAL EXPERIENCES

CHAPTER ONE

The Spiritual and Intellectual Journey

To regret one's own experiences is to arrest one's development. To deny one's own experiences is to put a lie into the
lips of one's life. It is no less than a denial of the soul.

OSCAR WILDE

The decision to include my experiences as part of this book was not an easy one; neither was the process of going through the pain of reconstructing many years of varied experiences. However, because the ideas for this book originated in my personal, educational and professional life, it is essential for me to include these experiences to show the roots of the intellectual and spiritual development of my work. The seeds for this book lie in my doctoral thesis.[1] Reflection on these experiences also shows how the study can be considered a link between the past and the future and between the individual and the society.

Although personal experiences are 'personal,' when we as human beings reflect on them and share them with others, we realize to what extent our personal experiences are intermingled and interconnected with the 'other' and with the experiences of society. We start to see the common ground that we share with others, and the similarity of our experiences. By sharing our personal experiences we also realize the uniqueness of each individual's experiences. Reflection on my personal experiences helped me first realize, and then develop, my dialectical thinking, which in turn helped me in going back and forth between my intellectual and spiritual experiences, between the East and the West, and between the experiences of society and the community and my personal stories. When reflecting on and narrating my personal stories, I learned how to construct and reconstruct past experiences in the light of new knowledge. I realized that we human beings make meaning out of our experiences, and that is such an essential part of being human. We live through many experiences, but if we do not reflect on them and reconstruct their meaning (and we usually do not), they by-pass our consciousness and are stored in the subconscious until an event triggers them and brings them back to life. So reflection on personal experiences has always helped me to understand and value the stories on my journey as important and worthwhile in my spiritual and intellectual development. Polanyi says,

> As human beings, we must inevitably see the universe from a center lying within us and speak it in terms of a human language shaped by the exigencies of human intercourse. Any attempt rigorously to elimi-nate our human perspective from our picture of the world must lead to absurdity.[2]

If we do not value our experiences that are deep within ourselves, we will always feel estranged and alien to ourselves. And as Oscar Wilde rightly said, denial of our experiences will be like the denial of the soul. We as spiritual beings know what denial of the soul means. We know the pain of separation that is caused by denial of the soul. I realized the importance of reflection on personal experiences and have included them in my writings and my research since I was a doctoral student at the University of Toronto. As I was doing my studies there, I realized that I was denying my soul and my spiritual experiences and separating them from my intellectual experiences and my professional life, as if I had two separate lives. I will elaborate on this issue later in this chapter to share with the reader the confusion and pain caused by such denial.

Research and thinking are always based on personal concerns. Even when the issues that preoccupy us, as researchers, are mainly social, political, spiritual, or affect humanity in general, there are always high-ly personal reasons why these more universal issues mean so much to us. Since 1988 I have kept asking myself why I am preoccupied by Islamic epistemology and Islamic education. I never had a particular interest in Islamic issues. I had always been a practicing Muslim, and I was brought up in a conservative Muslim home by loving and caring open-minded parents. So religion was not an issue for me. I accepted it and practiced it as part of my daily life.

Only in 1988, when I started reflecting on my personal experiences, did I realize that I was becoming preoccupied with Islamic issues and Islamic education because my Islamic religious identity was challenged at the University. Only then did I understand the importance of my religion to me. I also saw that I had been taking my religion for granted. When it was challenged, I became protective and defensive. Although Islam did not need my protection and defense, I was protecting my Islamic identity and my spirituality, the sacred knowledge kept in my soul and stored quietly in my consciousness.

From narrating my stories to myself and reflecting on them, I became aware of the importance of narrative inquiry as a research method that enables us as writers and researchers to shed some light on our personal experiences. By doing so, we reconstruct our experiences and create meanings that help us understand, value, and appreciate those experiences or reject them consciously and try to deal with them at the conscious level. What is certainly true is that we trust certain methods of research and reflection because they make sense to us, because they shed light on issues that are personally important to us, possibly even because they lend themselves naturally to researching and reconstructing personal experiences. For reflection on personal experiences, I relied on narrative inquiry as a simple yet profound method of analysis.

I believe some readers will have reservations about or even objection to including the personal experiences of an unknown author in a scholarly book. The reservation, I believe, is rooted in the traditional school of thinking that separates the personal from the professional and the subjective from the objective. It might be worth reminding readers that the major theme of this book is to promote an alternative holistic paradigm for developing holistic education, an education that addresses the personal as an essential part of the professional as one whole entity. The issues of subjectivity and objectivity are discussed in detail in later chapters. As Morgan states:

> There is a contribution of knowledge if the researcher can identify generic process or patterns through which human beings construct and make sense of their realities...The evidence generated by interpretive

research is much more likely to be of an evocative rather than comprehensive kind, to be sustained, rejected, or refined through future studies. The conclusions of one study merely provide a starting point in a
continuing cycle of inquiry.3

Believing in the power of revealing personal experiences as a means
for reconstructing one's knowledge, I am applying what I am preach-
ing about and starting with myself as the first step in applying an
alternative paradigm and moving away from the conventional positivist paradigm.

I am well aware that I am not al-Ghazālī, Muhammad Iqbal,
Heidegger, or any great thinker when including my personal experiences in a scholarly book. However, I am an ordinary scholar who has
been troubled by fragmented teaching methods and research methodology in both schools and universities and has tried to discover the
causes for such disenchantment. I also believe that the majority in any
academic or professional world are ordinary hard-working people
who are trying to make sense of the reality around them. So ordinary
people can relate to one another's experiences and benefit from them.

When I had the intellectual and spiritual conflict in 1988, I did not
know that reflecting on past experiences and retelling my childhood
stories might help in understanding the roots of the conflict that are
deeply buried in my childhood. In childhood the foundations are laid
for the disposition of the mind. Why do we humans think in the way
we do? It is not all due to adult experience and university training. Our
early childhood biography surely has something to do with it. Stories
prove that much more is hidden in our lives than we first realize. We
have to be taught to take our own experiences seriously. I am convinced that hidden in our lives are springs that, if tapped at the right
time, can quench the thirst to discover the source for our struggle,
pain, and conflict.

A direct contact with our own life stories is for us a way to self-
knowledge and, beyond that, an entry to wisdom. Thus, any event is
contingent on a narrative, and any single narrative is contingent on a
wider narrative context. This wider narrative context comes from
one's history, traditions, religion, and the society or community of
people with whom we share our narrative. To look at narrative outside

a wider narrative context or outside the shared history of society is both misleading and pointless. As Muslims, our personal and separate stories, if shared and shaped by the larger Islamic narrative context, can provide the new generation with a wealth of personal experiences to which they can relate. This encourages them to reflect on their personal experiences and place them in the larger Islamic context. The Muslims' historical memory of colonization is not fixed, nor is my personal memory of episodes related to colonization and the damage done to the structure of the Islamic Ummah and Islamic society in the past and the present.

Histography is a form of social memory and held to be irrelevant to personal memory by modern psychology. Yet, arguably, modern psychology has damaged the human mind and soul by applying irresponsible, inhumane theories and inquiry methods. The meaning of any story is rooted in history and a social group, not just in the personal mind. Stories always take on their meaning in relationship to other stories, some of which are rooted in the collective memory of the community. "Narrative collections are part of the knowledge that glues any culture together. Collections of stories to which we have access and with which we agree, establish our faith in the social system in which we believe."4

Therefore, by rooting my ideas of Islamic epistemology in my personal experiences, I am aiming at contributing to the Muslim collective memory by reflection on personal experiences. I am also aiming to anchor my intellectual and spiritual experiences in my Islamic upbringing to mirror the unity of knowledge and oneness of experience. Spirituality has always been an essential part of my life since childhood but I never thought about it or labeled it as such, so I never considered myself a spiritual person. There was harmony between mind, body and soul. That harmony was severely disrupted by several factors, one of which was the deep feeling of separation between mind and soul that I experienced in my doctoral program at the University.

By reflecting on personal experiences, I also want to encourage students and scholars to follow the golden thread of their spiritual experience and to bring to life the wholeness and holiness of their Islamic identity, or lack of identity for that matter. Muslim students can contribute actively in constructing and reconstructing Islamic knowledge not only by choosing topics related to the Islamic Ummah but also, more importantly, by using research methods that are rooted in the Islamic paradigm and by interpreting their studies from an Islamic perspective and within an Islamic paradigm.

FRAGMENTATION AND WHOLENESS

When I first decided to include a chapter on my personal experiences in this book, I divided the chapter into two sections: (1) the intellectual journey; and (2) the spiritual journey. As I was trying to separate the events and experiences to categorize them, I felt somehow disturbed inside, and could not determine the source of that feeling. I felt frustrated because of the difficulty of separating the experiences. Suddenly, I realized that the discomfort created by this continuing tension was because of my attempts to separate my mind from my soul. I had been struggling against this conflict since 1988. Fragmentation of self and knowledge is a major theme of this book that I am trying to explain; my goal is to avoid it in the education system and in my personal and professional life. Yet, I myself kept falling into the trap of separation, categorization and fragmentation.

My scientific training of categorizing, analyzing, and objectifying kept invading my writing and my reflections. I realized that there was no separation between my soul and my mind. My spiritual and intellectual journeys were one, and the intermingling of these two had made me who I was. I never considered myself a religious or spiritual person. I was an ordinary Muslim woman who lived her life to some extent according to the Islamic laws. However, when I started reflecting on my personal experiences, I realized to what extent all my childhood and adulthood were engulfed in religiosity and spirituality. As my sisters, brothers and I were sent to school to develop and discipline our young minds, our souls were disciplined and protected from worldly pollution by our parents. So both my mind and soul were growing in harmony. God was introduced into my life in childhood. Every event and every celebration was based on religious concepts, whether it was a happy celebration of life like the two Eids, Ramadan, marriage, and birth, or sad occasions like sickness, calamities, or

death. Everything was a religious activity, and everything was analyzed and understood from a religious perspective. God was always at
the center of our activities and hence the center of our beings. We were
always taught, not in so many words, though, that God was the center
and the core, that we came from God, and that we should go back to
him. My spiritual life was developed and nurtured by my parents and
reinforced by society. Religion and spirituality are not only a personal
matter, as both the West and the East (the communist bloc) have tried
to convince themselves and others. Although communicating with
God, meditating and praying are personal matters, they are also social
matters. If the community in which we live is so far away from religiosity and spirituality, then spiritual development will either diminish and disappear or will be challenged and developed even more.
Being religious and spiritual means being virtuous and ethical and following God's guidance to fulfill our mission in this temporary passage
to eternity. Leading an ethical life, no doubt, will reflect on the individual, and on society, too.

By reflecting on my personal experience, I realized that my Islamic
worldview and belief system had been growing within me since childhood. A worldview does not come out of a vacuum. It grows like a
tree, and if it is nurtured with love, care, and knowledge, it grows and
gives healthy fruit. Love is an essential component for spiritual development. Some unfortunate children have been introduced to Islamic
religion with fear and terror, which has made them resent religion,
God, and the spiritual side of their beings. They may deny their soul,
forget it, bury it in the depths of their unconsciousness, and increase
their own alienation from themselves and from reality.

WEAVING THE BELIEF SYSTEM INTO ONE'S BEING

By reclaiming my childhood from reflection on my experiences, I
could trace the roots of my belief system (worldview) and how it was
created. I came to realize then what had created such a strong Islamic
worldview inside me: a belief system that was whole. What is certainly
true is that at a young age one cannot realize the depth of those experiences and how effortless they were then, as if they had been hand-
woven into our being since childhood, thread by thread. I was living

my life peacefully, without having to worry about defending or protecting my Islamic identity. My parents carried that responsibility.

My Islamic identity, however, was challenged at the University of Toronto. I could not have experienced this reality if I had not gone through a spiritual and intellectual crisis as I was doing my doctoral degree. I realized later that the endless hours that I spent in the libraries, looking for and reading all kinds of books, were in fact not so much a search for references, but for my Islamic and holistic identity. I understood that I was trying to legitimize my whole being: mind, soul, and body. In the search for my identity, I was forced to answer difficult questions. At one point, I felt that I had to choose between my two sides, the spiritual or the intellectual. The choice was a brutal one, which could result in the separation of the mind and the soul. I realized at that point that the situation was out of my control and beyond my ability to solve. I took refuge in God and begged for His help. By continual reflection, contemplation, and constant prayers to God Almighty to clarify things for me, I survived that intellectual and spiritual crisis and realized that oneness and unity in self and knowledge was what I should be seeking for the rest of my life. Only then did I have a sense of wholeness again.

The seeds of this book were planted in 1988, when I was going through a hard and challenging time of the separation and reunion of my soul and mind. The importance of this lies not only in the fact that what is personal is real and intense and it shakes our whole internal being, but also in the universality of our experiences as students from an Islamic background and their effect on our perception of vital issues that threaten our identity as Muslims. I should like to invite all graduate students to reflect on their experiences, to focus on the tensions that are created in their lives, to treasure those tensions and embrace them instead of resenting them, to be able to go beyond the stress and the tensions, and redirect the inner tensions to a mission or a goal that they are striving to achieve. I am well aware that people achieve their goals by following different routes, and this is only one route that led me to many profound horizons of knowledge and love.

CHAPTER TWO

Spirituality: Woman's Best-Kept Secret

Since in Islam the intellect (*al-ʿaql*) and the spirit (*al-rūḥ*) are closely related, the acquiring of knowledge itself has always been seen as a religious activity. In fact supreme knowledge is identified with the highest spiritual realization, and Islamic spirituality as a whole possesses a sapiential and gnostic character. That is why the Islamic doctrines on the nature of Reality or the knowledge of Reality constitute a basic element of Islamic spirituality.[1]

Spirituality and intellectuality are, indeed, closely related in Islam and together they form the unique aspect of the wholeness of Islamic epistemology. Knowledge according to Islamic epistemology is not restricted to the intellect only, for certain dimensions of knowledge are realized by the soul. Since the thesis of this book is to promote Islamic holistic education by analyzing and understanding the roots and multidimensionality of Islamic epistemology and applying them to education, I believe that it is appropriate to include a chapter on spirituality. Having said that, I believe that it is more appropriate for me as a woman to present spirituality from the woman's perspective rather than writing about the subject in general. Reviewing the literature reveals the fact that most of the writing on Islamic spirituality is produced by men and naturally represents spirituality from the male perspective.

I should like to clarify at this point that the aim of writing on woman's spirituality is not to advance any feminine ideology nor to undermine what is written on the subject by male authors. On the contrary, the aim is simple and legitimate and falls within the objective of this book, namely, to develop an alternative paradigm that helps in producing Islamic knowledge which is whole and takes into consideration the wholeness of life, the subjective and the objective, the male and the female, the *yin* and the *yang*. Some readers may wonder if this book is on epistemology or on woman's psychology. Reminding ourselves of one issue as we read the book will help us to keep track of ideas and appreciate the relevance of issues that might seem remote from the topic. We have to remember that we are discussing the issue of wholeness in Islamic education and epistemology. This means that both intellectuality and spirituality must be included. Both spirituality and psychology deal with issues related to the inner aspects of one's being: although there are differences between *al-nafs* and *al-rūḥ*, at certain levels they are related.

It might be worth mentioning here that what is presented in this chapter does not exclude men from following the same path of spiritual development. However, because of the differences in the nature of men and women and because of social and cultural demands and upbringing, men, especially in the East, are taught from an early age to be tough and not to show emotions and feelings because that will affect their manhood. So naturally, men and women have different perceptions of all issues in life and spirituality is one of them. Since this book is about Islamic epistemology, theories of knowledge, and ways of knowing, it is appropriate to present the woman's spirituality to mirror the religious and sacred dimension of Islamic spirituality as a holistic way of knowing from the woman's perspective.

In my quest to understand woman's spirituality from an Islamic perspective, I came across three Eastern sources that helped me to analyze my ideas of what I call 'practical spirituality.' These three sources were (1) Rābiʿah's mystical journey; (2) al-Ghazālī's theory of virtue; and (3) the Chinese concept of the fundamental forces of *yin* and *yang*. Rābiʿah, however, was an inspiration for my ideas of practical spirituality.

When my mind was in a state of confusion and chaos in trying to understand and make meaning of woman's spirituality, I thought that Rabiʿah's spirituality and her mystical journey would embody Muslim women's spirituality and that, by understanding her, I should be able to explain and bring to life woman's spirituality. After reading books written on and about Rābiʿah, I was even more confused. I could not relate to her profound mystical experiences. At the same time, I was sure that there was another level or another dimension of spirituality experienced by most Muslim women, both professional and nonprofessional. Rābiᶜah's mystical experience was unique and exceptional. However, what I should like to depict here is the spirituality of millions of Muslim women who are practicing and experiencing spirituality every day while struggling with mundane practical issues. Practical spirituality is a challenge for the ordinary Muslim woman who wants to live according to Islamic teachings in the twenty-first century. I shared my confusion about Rābiᶜah's mystical experiences and my simple spiritual experiences, that I later called 'practical spirituality,' with my friend, Dr. Furlong. Having been on that mystical journey for so long, she replied immediately:

> I know what you mean about the challenge of writing things that we feel are common sense. Common sense is really intuition and thus it is invisible or implicit/tacit knowledge for which we don't have a lot of everyday language.
>
> I wrote about mysticism as being an everyday experience only we have made it mysterious and relegated it to special relationships that only a few have with God. However, when we go past all the mysteries, the myths that religions and cultures have created, and our own preconceived ideas, we learn that in the moments of meeting others, the cosmos and ourselves soul to soul.
>
> When we stop looking with our minds and open our souls to the other (people of the cosmos) we touch the face of God; The Universal love flowing through all existence that we know without words when we touch it or it touches us. The mother gazing on her newborn child, the elder lifting a rose gently in her hand, the lover looking into the soul of her beloved and seeing the transparency of her own soul, the singer giving her soul song to the universe, the caretaker nurturing the healing of the sufferer, the listener hearing the breeze move through the leaves, the bird whistling to creation, the ocean ebbing and flowing just for the sake of it, the writer crafting a gift of silent knowledge for all of us to learn, the friend always present through the light and dark times.[2]

Spirituality is one of the most profound ways of intuitive knowing. It is a silent yet powerful way of knowing. Facts and numbers cannot prove intuition, unlike reasoning and rationality. It is either felt internally or it is not. Woman, because of the innate qualities that God gave her, is more prepared to admit and accept her intuitive feelings and knowing. That of course does not mean that men do not experience spiritual development. They do, but it is different and perceived also differently. Spirituality is an inner feeling that cannot be proven by facts or reason. Only recently in some academic circles has intuition been accepted as an alternative way of knowing. In general, nothing can compete with rationality and reasoning in male-dominated societies in both the East and the West. However, that does not mean that men are intellectual and women are spiritual. That is a very naive and simplistic analysis of what I am trying to present here. Any issue should be presented from different angles so as to be perceived holistically. Woman has kept her way of knowing to herself, realizing its power and reliability, though it is not accepted and honored in academic institutes controlled by men. Spirituality and intuition are parallel and one leads to the other. Believing in her intuition and nurturing it, woman prepares her inner self to grow and listen to the sacred inside her. Gradually she discovers that what is inside her is more than mere intuition or the 'sixth sense,' as it is called sometimes. She becomes more sensitive, more receptive, more loving, and more caring. She realizes that her soul is moving within her, asking her to look inside to see the source of the beauty and ecstasy she has been experiencing.

When the soul is given the right surroundings in which to grow and experience its sacredness, the person who treasures the soul inwardly becomes spiritual. The majority of women who live in a Muslim community have surroundings that encourage and support the development of one's spirituality. A Muslim woman keeps this secret to herself. She grows through her spirituality silently as she experiences the joy and pain of life. From early childhood she learns that she can take refuge in God if the world treats her viciously. She is in touch with her inner self from a very early age. Very few books have been written on Muslim woman's spirituality and even fewer have been written by Muslim spiritual women themselves. It appears that these women regard their spirituality as a private matter; I personally do. Religiosity can be a public matter, but not spirituality. The difference between the two is that religious rituals are only a manifestation of a deeper level of inner realization.

That deeper level of knowing and realization is what I call spiritual. When the meaning of God's words suddenly bursts inside our souls and we feel that the divine words are shaking the depths of our being, only then do we feel elevated and transformed. That state I call spiritual. When I feel the ocean of God's love flooding my soul and my whole being, I feel ecstatic and holy. That state becomes part of my identity, my being. However, when we women are just starting our spiritual journey, consciously or subconsciously, this state of elevation makes us fragile and transparent. We set out on the journey to the inner path, not knowing where we are heading. We follow a light that is inside us and is called *al-fiṭra*, primordial. We make the journey with confidence in God's Divine Words and His Grace. Since childhood we have recited and read the Divine Book, but at that young age, it does not necessarily touch the depths of the soul. The more we reflect on those words, the deeper we go and the closer we come to the path. The degree of our sincerity, our capability to realize the depth of those words and our innate ability to love and receive love are reflected in the level of spirituality that we attain. As woman grows and experiences more spiritual meaning in her life, she becomes stronger and feels empowered by her spirituality. She feels more confident in herself and in the path that she has chosen to travel. She reaches the stage where she knows that she knows. She starts trusting her knowledge and uses her intuitive knowledge in solving daily problems and even making decisions. She trusts that knowledge because it comes from the soul and she knows that her soul is connected to the Universal soul.

It is the sacred inside us that yearns for the Sacred and seeks the Sacred. Thus, a Muslim woman's spirituality is rooted in religion. Religious virtues, however, can be transformed into the mystical or spiritual level when our obedience to God and His Divine Commandment goes beyond fear of punishment and hope for reward: those virtues are transformed into pure love. Humility and modesty are transformed into dignity and pride. What makes the transformation of virtues possible is the concept of *tawḥīd*, oneness and unity. Having believed in God's Oneness, a Muslim woman can bridge the distance between virtues and go beyond the many to the One and Absolute.

All virtues discussed by Muslim philosophers, theologians, scientists, and mystics are derived, more or less directly, from the Divine Book. Al-Ghazālī's list of mystical virtues is given in Table 2.1. Al-Ghazālī, of course, deals with mystical virtues as essentially based on the Islamic religious tradition. "In his view these mystical virtues are nothing but the interpretation of the hidden meanings of the divine commandments."3 Practical spirituality is the implementation of the Divine Commandments at two levels, this world and the hereafter. The religious virtues are what constitute virtuous and moral human beings that can live their lives according to the moral code of that religion as well as attaining the means for the hereafter. Being aware of religious and mystical virtues, woman can achieve higher levels of spirituality at the earlier stages of her life.

By encouraging the practice of religious rituals from an early age, parents start disciplining their children's souls to receive God's love, grace, and teachings. If, for example, we as Muslims examine daily prayers for the apparent meaning (ẓāhir) and the hidden meaning (bāṭin), we realize that they develop the inner self by continual repentance (tawbah) of our wrong-doing and thus we express our humility in front of God. During our prayers, every time we prostrate ourselves physically in front of the Creator, we actually discipline the ego inside us to be humble and to remind ourselves that we are only God's powerless servants. At the same time, we are also reminded that we are God's vicegerents on earth. Every time we pronounce ashhadu an lā ilāha illā Allāh wa ashhadu anna Muḥammadan rasūl Allāh, or what we call the shahādatayn, we testify that there is no god but Allah and that Muhammad is his servant and his messenger. Five times a day we are reminded of who we are, who we can be, and the potential that we have for knowing God by knowing ourselves.

AL-GHAZĀLĪ'S THEORY OF VIRTUE AND SPIRITUALITY

Love, in the broad meaning of the word, is the source of woman's spirituality, although it is manifested in many different ways. Woman, compared with man, is by nature more sensitive, caring, intuitive,

Al-Ghazālī's list of virtues in Iḥyā' ʿUlūm al-Dīn4
[Table 2.1]

WISDOM	COURAGE	TEMPERANCE	JUSTICE
Discretion	Magnificence	Liberality	—
Excellence of discernment	Intrepidity	Modesty	—
Penetration of ideas	Manliness	Patience	—
Correctness of opinion	Greatness of soul	Remission	—
Awareness of subtle actions and mysteries of the evils of the soul	Endurance	Contentment	—
	Gentleness	Abstinence	—
	Fortitude	Contentment	—
	Suppression of anger	Honest dealing	—
	Correct evaluation of self	Wit	—
	Amiability, etc.	Righteous indignation	—

emotional, and more spiritual. Ancient Eastern Chinese thinkers attested this fact, and so have Western scientific studies. Woman possesses more qualities that belong to the heart and soul. I do not have to defend woman and say that she has brains too – that is common sense. God created woman as the bearer and nurturer of an innocent child who resides inside her. She is given this extra gift of sensitivity and intuition to help her take care of another soul inside her. Woman starts listening to the heartbeat of her child with her soul even before the heart of that child actually starts beating. What I am trying to explain here is what makes woman's spiritual experiences unique and different from man's spirituality, and probably more profound.

Love is the source of spirituality for all human beings. It is certainly so for woman because from the Creation woman has been known for her soft-heartedness, her compassion, her love, and her caring attitude. God created woman so that she would be more loving, caring, and nurturing, and He assigned her different roles in life. As woman passes through the stages of motherhood, she develops and refines her feminine qualities even more. She is honored and given this privilege of carrying another soul inside her. When God breathes His Spirit into the child, woman's spirituality is intensified as she feels the body and the soul of the child. Woman experiences intense love as her child grows inside her, and that love grows even more when that child is born. No man can claim such a strong and intense love for his children, no matter how much he cares for and loves them. Motherhood allows woman to experience different dimensions of her being and higher levels of love. Selfless love is a profound dimension of love, and woman is privileged to go through the experience of selfless love for her child. Experiencing such an intense love develops woman's spirituality one step further to be able to go beyond the love of the relative to the love of the Absolute.

PATIENCE AND ENDURANCE

Another virtue suggested by al-Ghazālī as a mystical virtue is patience (*ṣabr*), which is also related to love. Patience is not possessed exclusively by women, but it is associated with motherhood and the trouble and pain that mothers undergo while bringing up their children. Patience helps a woman to develop her spirituality further. A mother's patience is tested as her children go through sickness, hard times, and the challenges of life.

GRATITUDE AND THANKSGIVING

Gratitude (*shukr*) is another mystical virtue that motherhood intensifies, although it, too, is experienced by both men and women. The key word is not men nor women; it is the gentleness of the heart that is open to give and receive love. Yet, because of woman's unique

God-given qualities, especially her gentle heart, she experiences all mystical virtues more intensely and more profoundly, because they are associated with love. When woman gives thanks to God for the many blessings that her child is enjoying, or for the child's success in life, that gratitude comes from the bottom of her soul. She expresses her gratitude to God with her tears and by praying, helping the needy and the poor, or celebrating with friends and family. No matter what form the celebration takes, it is spiritually based, so that woman's soul is elevated and purified day after day.

TRUST

Trust (*tawakkul*) is presented by al-Ghazālī together with Divine Unity (*tawḥīd*). Al-Ghazālī maintains that Divine Unity is the basis for trust. Divine Unity is the knowledge that produces trust. Woman in her state of motherhood goes through many difficult times, not only with her child, but also with her husband and sometimes with herself, too. Woman learns from her spiritual journey on the inner path, that she has no choice but to be patient and to trust that God will take care of things: she must trust Him completely and leave the problems in His hands after trying her best. As woman goes through stages of spirituality, she realizes that some problems have no solutions and that she has to accept the situation, painful as it may be, for every life has pain and disappointment. Deceiving ourselves by pretending that we humans can solve all our problems and that things are under our control is illusory, unrealistic, and far from spirituality.

CHASTITY, DIGNITY, AND EMPOWERMENT

Islamic literature contains hundreds of books written by both traditional and contemporary theologians, philosophers, and mystics on the inner interpretation of Qur'anic virtues and the Divine Commandments. Because living according to the Divine Commandments increases the likelihood of receiving God's blessings (*barakah*), these commandments become the means of teaching virtues in the Islamic community. One of the religious virtues that can transform woman's religiosity to spirituality is chastity (*ʿiffah*). Chastity, a powerful religious virtue, is associated with woman's way of life and her relationships, especially with men. The virtue of chastity empowers woman with a divine dignity that is reflected in her appearance and her code of dress as an initial step, and then is transformed to inner qualities of self-control, dignity, serenity, and absolute submission to God's words.

A Muslim woman feels empowered and transformed by her spirituality. Practicing Islamic rituals and observing the Divine Commandments empower woman and provide her with the necessary tools to operate in today's society on her own terms. Spirituality can be equated with dignity, empowerment, caring, and gentleness. Preserving her spirituality, woman has enough confidence not to go out of her way to play the man's role, to compete with him on his terms, or to fight for her rights. A spiritual woman starts her journey from a religious and ethical basis. She continues her growth and development where her parents left off. They began disciplining her soul with religious and philosophical virtues, and she has transformed those virtues to mystical virtues. Woman feels empowered by her strong connection with God. She answers to Him and begs from Him. Her humility, modesty, and need are for Him alone. Operating at this high level, the Muslim woman never humiliates herself before another human being. Her humility to God puts her on a high pedestal. Her awareness of God's knowledge and love of him dignifies her. She *knows* no one can provide her with or deprive her of anything if God does not wish it. So she knows her need is only for God's grace (*barakah*), love, and His compassion.

Every spiritual journey is unique, and it is influenced by various social, political, and religious factors as well as the innate qualities of the individual. Woman's spiritual training starts from childhood as she is introduced to the various rituals of praying, fasting, reciting the Qur'an, and participating in religious events. As a child, she accepts the disciplining of her soul openly because her mind is not yet harmed by the education system that imposes the separation of mind and soul. She accepts all the teachings because it is in accordance with her instinct (*fiṭra*), which is pure and, if trained properly, leads to the Divine Path. However, as the body, mind, and soul develop, we humans are exposed to many contradictory sources of knowledge that can influence the direction and development of our growth.

SPIRITUALITY AND THE WISDOM OF *YIN* AND *YANG*

From the wisdom of the Tao, I learned the concept of wholeness, one-ness, polarity, and complementarity. Such wisdom teaches that life is dynamic, and that its changing patterns arise from *yang* and *yin*, forces or polar principles found throughout nature. We know them as day and night, heat and cold, male and female, action and repose. One extreme complements, even contains, the other. Action and repose seem opposite, but wise action includes rest, reflection, and inner guidance, avoiding the extremes of compulsiveness (excessive *yang*) or passivity (excessive *yin*). The dynamic balance of these forces brings harmony and tranquility to the mind, body, and soul in both nature and ourselves.

The main theme of this book is wholeness and holiness. It will be proposed in later chapters how wholeness and holiness can be achieved from an Islamic, holistic paradigm. The issue of keeping the balance between the intellectual and spiritual dimensions of oneself will be considered in detail. In this chapter on woman's spirituality, I am sharing with the reader what I learned from the Chinese wisdom of wholeness, oneness, and harmony, from the complementary concepts of *yin* and *yang*. The twelfth-century Chinese philosopher Chu Hsi explained that the phase of repose was *yin*, the phase of activity was *yang*, and this perpetual alternation of *yin* and *yang* in its turn produced the five elements: water, earth, metal, fire, and wood. From the five elements, heaven and earth were derived, and from them all creation.5 The Tao teaches that "all life embodies *yin* and embraces *yang*" (*Tao* 42). All existence, the microcosm and the macrocosm, emerges from the synthesis of the forces, which stems from the Primal Being. As *yin* simultaneously *contrasts* with and embraces *yang*, their interaction produces a new creation.

WOMAN'S SPIRITUALITY AND *YIN* QUALITIES

Although human beings possess both *yin* and *yang* qualities, woman generally possesses more *yin*. In the Chinese literature *yin* is characterized in a multitude of ways: as darkness, moon, night, winter, earth, valley, water, open, soft, interior, contracting, passive, contemplative, feminine, nurturing, feeling, listening, intuition, unconscious, repose, and knowing. *Yang*, the complement of *yin*, is described as follows: light, sun, day, summer, heaven, mountain, stone, closed, hard, excess, exterior, expanding, aggressive, active, masculine, achieving, thinking, speaking, reason, conscious, action, and doing.

Some of the *yin* qualities essential for spirituality have to be earned by man, although woman possesses them. They are innate to her gentle nature: qualities like intuition, softness, interiority, passiveness, contemplation, nurturing, feeling, knowing, listening, and repose. In reflecting on *yin* qualities, I have realized that some of the qualities that look negative are only symbolic. Darkness and night, for example, represent woman's mystery. Throughout history, woman has been seen in her mysterious characteristics. 'Passive' represents her quietness, serenity, and modesty. Spirituality is a journey on the inner path. It is internal, quiet, and intuitive. Spirituality does not need outward action or aggression.

Muslim women, like all women in the world, have been subjected to men's tyranny and aggression. Yet Muslim women's religiosity and spirituality have, in most cases, saved them from self-deception or being deceived by men. Muslim women, generally, have not permitted men to strip away their femininity, families, or friends. Above all, they have not allowed men to take God out of their lives, because God is the center and core of any Muslim woman's life. I am well aware of many Muslim women who choose to live secular lives, but I am talking about practicing Muslim women.

I have asked myself many times what it is that makes a Muslim woman strong and empowered despite all the aggression around her. After long hours of reflection and soul-searching, I have realized that it might be her spirituality that has saved her. Because of the traditional and religious upbringing of girls in an Islamic society, God is introduced into a woman's life in childhood, so religion is a genuine part of her being and her identity. We humans are alarmed when anything touches our identity, and we do whatever it takes to protect it. Spirituality is an inner dimension of woman's identity; it is invisible. Religion has never been considered the enemy in Muslim societies, as the church has been in the West. The Muslim woman has clung to her religion as a safe haven to protect her from the world's aggression. This world for Muslims is only a temporary world, a transit to the hereafter. However, it is in this world that we humans have to do the good deeds to see the results in the hereafter. So when woman's goal is beyond the physical and the visible and her aspirations are beyond the material gain, she has nothing to lose. Her need is for God's love, God's knowledge, and God's blessings. That is why I believe that spirituality is the Muslim woman's best-kept secret. Her love for God, her prayers, and meditation or contemplation are private. Privacy is a characteristic of the Muslim woman. She keeps her problems with others to herself. She complains to God and prays to God to help her. She neither goes public nor seeks the advice of psychotherapists. She goes directly to God, asks guidance, help, and endurance. Those private moments are the most intense spiritual moments that woman can experience. Being soft and open and accepting her vulnerability and weakness, woman bursts into tears and cries while communicating with God. She does not shy away from her weakness. It is in those moments of her soul meeting with God that new meanings of life are realized. She understands and accepts. She *knows* it is right because she knows that God is touching her soul.

The Muslim woman, who is connected to God and seeks understanding and love from Him, emerges stronger from her painful experiences. She feels empowered by God's grace and His blessings. She reaches the stage where nothing matters any more but God's satisfaction (*riḍā*). Despite the modesty and humbleness of those moments, woman realizes and transcends her pain in loving. Through pain she is transformed. Her frustration, anger, feelings of injustice and betrayal become the joy of pleasing God. If this is what He wants, then so be it. She knows her reward (*thawāb*) is given somewhere else, in higher realms.

II
REVIEW AND CRITIQUE

CHAPTER THREE

Conventional and Alternative Paradigms

A paradigm is a model which we, as humans, use to understand the world. It comprises certain philosophical assumptions that guide thinking and action. Based on the philosophical assumptions, it contains epistemological and methodological assumptions. Therefore a worldview that one develops over the years is derived from that paradigm, and it can be microscopic or telescopic. A microscopic worldview or paradigm is limited and possibly narrow-minded. It aims at discovering details of the object it examines. A telescopic worldview or paradigm is farsighted and open and permits close-ups of the object under study, yet in a large context. Guba identifies three questions that help define a paradigm:

1. The ontological question is *what is the nature of reality?*
2. The epistemological question is *what is the nature of knowledge and the relationship between the knower and the known?*
3. The methodological question is, *how can the knower go about obtaining the desired knowledge and understanding?*[1]

In this chapter the aim is to shed some light on existing paradigms to prepare the ground for the Islamic paradigm. First, positivism is presented as the dominant paradigm. Second, the interpretive/constructivist paradigm is presented as an alternative paradigm. Third, the continuing debate between quantitative and qualitative research methods is presented to make students aware of major issues related to existing paradigms. Finally, the criteria for qualitative research are presented for validating alternative research methods and inquiry.

The purpose of presenting conventional and alternative paradigms

at this point is to set the stage for the Islamic paradigm, Islamic education, and Islamic methodology. All Muslim students, graduates and
undergraduates studying at universities in North America and Europe, are using either conventional or alternative methods of inquiry.
However, one should ask how many of those students are aware of
their own paradigm and worldview, and the relationship between the
methodology that they are using and their philosophical assumptions
about the nature of reality that guide their thinking and research. One
should also ask why students should be aware of such a relationship,
as long as their work is solid, reliable, and valid.

If Muslim scholars in the East and the West are concerned about the
production and advancement of Islamic knowledge, then they should
be concerned first about awakening Muslim students' awareness of the
latter's worldviews. A Muslim student who comes from a practicing
conservative family and who is a practicing Muslim, might blindly produce highly valid and scholarly research on cloning or genetic engineering which might cause a great deal of harm to humanity; ultimately
such a project might deeply scar her or his belief system. Scientifically it
would be sound research, but religiously and morally it might be dangerous and improper. The discrepancy between a religious paradigm
and a secular, positivist methodology creates internal confusion and
struggle for the researcher. The conflict is between belief and action,
between believing in one thing and doing something else. From an
Islamic point of view and in the Qur'an, knowledge (ʿilm) and action
(ʿamal) are always associated with each other to remind us, as Muslims, to be consistent in what we say and what we do. Such a reminder
helps us, as teachers, to keep the balance between theory and practice;
between what we preach and what we practice in both our professional
and personal lives.

Therefore, if one of the aims of research is to build a body of
knowledge that reflects and represents Islamic traditions and contributes to the reconstruction of Islamic science, then Muslim students
would do well to be aware of the potential and shortcomings of existing paradigms so as to be familiar with the Islamic paradigm and its
potential for developing an Islamic body of knowledge as it did more
than fourteen centuries ago. The reader might think that if we, as

researchers, are to be objective, we have to be aware of the shortcomings of the Islamic paradigm too, because obviously any paradigm has advantages and disadvantages. I could not agree more. However, in comparing existing paradigms and the Islamic paradigm, we are comparing a man-made paradigm with one that is sent by God. The Islamic paradigm is derived directly from the Divine Book and based on Divine Principles. Every approach has advantages and disadvantages except God's way, which was revealed to the Seal of the Prophets, Muhammad. As a Muslim scholar and teacher, I can trust my students' souls and minds only to God's words and the Islamic paradigm.

THE POSITIVIST PARADIGM

The dominant paradigm that has guided educational and psychological research for many decades is positivism. Positivism is based on the rationalistic, empiricist philosophy that originated with Francis Bacon, John Locke, and Auguste Comte. The underlying assumptions of positivism include the belief that the social world can be studied in the same way as the natural world, that there is a method for studying the social world that is value-free, and that explanations of causal nature can be provided. Positivism rests upon five assumptions summarized by Guba and Lincoln:

> an ontological assumption of a single, tangible, reality 'out there' that can be broken apart into pieces capable of being studied independently; the whole is simply being the sum of the parts; an epistemological assumption about the possibility of separation of the observer from the observed, the knower from the known; an assumption of the temporal and contextual independence of observations, so that what is true at one time and place may, under appropriate circumstances (such as sampling) also be true at another time and place; an assumption of linear causality, that there are no effects without causes and no causes without effects; an axiological assumption of value freedom, that is, that the methodology guarantees that the results of an inquiry are essentially free from the influence of any value system (bias).[2]

Thus, from an ontological point of view positivists hold that *one* reality exists and that it is the researcher's job to discover, to know that reality. The researcher and the subject of the study are assumed to be independent, that is, they do not influence each other.3 Positivists base their experimental methods on those of the natural and physical sciences, assuming that objects and human beings possess the same qualities and react in the same way under controlled conditions. Thus the researcher, in the positivist paradigm, attempts to have complete control over the conditions of the study by manipulating, changing, or holding constant external influences and by measuring a very limited set of outcome variables. Researchers, consciously or subconsciously, carry out a study, assuming that there is a single, tangible reality. They assume that they are capable of grasping that reality, provided that they follow some experimental and statistical protocols. They believe that by such procedures, they may delimit a problem so that it is measurable, and at the same time avoid fragmenting it. Ultimately, they seek to manipulate the situation and control it. The more detached the researcher is from the data and the 'subject' of the study, the more 'objective' he or she is in collecting and analyzing the data, and the more rigorous, valid, and reliable the results are considered to be. The results, then can be generalized, assuming that problems, situations, and circumstances are reproducible. Thus results are treated and are time and context free. Some of these generalizations are formulated as cause-and-effect laws. Yet the numerous limitations imposed by the paradigm on the research and consequently on the investigation of the problem and the gathering of the data prevent the positivist research methods from being open to and encompassing human complexities. Such investigations are intrinsically unable to analyze any situation holistically.

THE INTERPRETIVE/CONSTRUCTIVIST PARADIGM

Disenchantment with the positivist paradigm and knowledge produced by quantitative methods and analyzed statistically led social scientists to look for alternative research methods and paradigms. Many different labels have been used for the interpretive/constructivist paradigm. Tesch identifies twenty-five different types of qualitative research and evaluation methods that are closely associated with it.4 'Naturalistic inquiry' is an umbrella term that covers a number of such alternative research methods. The approach gained momentum in the 1970s and 1980s as a reaction to conventional approaches to research when these proved inadequate for understanding the complexity of educational problems. Alternative approaches to educational research and evaluation, as noted by Simons,[5] include holistic evaluation,[6] illuminative evaluation,[7] democratic evaluation,[8] evaluation as literary criticism,[9] transactional evaluation,[10] educational connoisseurship,[11] quasi-legal evaluation,[12] and naturalistic evaluation.[13]

The constructivist term was chosen for the paradigm because it reflects one of the basic assumptions, that is, reality is socially constructed. This paradigm emerged from the philosopher Edmund Husserl's phenomenology and Wilhelm Dilthey's study of interpretive or hermeneutic understanding in the human sciences.[14] Hermeneutics is the study of the interpretive understanding of meaning. Historians use the concept of hermeneutics in their discussion of biblical and historical documents to refer to the understanding of what the author was attempting to communicate within her or his cultural and temporal context. Interpretive researchers use the term more generally to interpret the meaning of something from a certain standpoint. The basic assumptions underlying the interpretive paradigm, identified by Guba and Lincoln are as follows:

> an ontological assumption of a multiple, constructed and holistic reality; realities exist in the form of multiple mental constructions; an epistemological assumption about the knower and the known as interactive and inseparable; an assumption of temporal and context dependence; only time-and context-bound, working hypotheses and ideographic statements are possible; an assumption of causality and that all entities are in a state of mutual simultaneous shaping, so that it is impossible to distinguish causes from effects; an axiological assumption that methodology is necessarily value bound, interactive, subjective and based on participants' views.[15]

Further issues related to the above paradigms are now discussed, with respect to ontology, epistemology, and methodology.

ONTOLOGY

The belief system of constructivism is rooted in a nonabsolutist ontology. Realities exist in the form of multiple mental constructions, socially and experientially based, dependent in their form and content on the people who hold them, some of which maybe in conflict with one another. So perception of reality may change during the study. Constructivists reject the notion that there is an objective reality that can be known and take the stance that the researcher's goal is to understand the multiple social constructions of meaning and knowledge. The value of empathy is emphasized in the interpretivist and phenomenological doctrine of *verstehen*, which undergirds many constructivists inquiries. *Verstehen*, a concept emphasized by Dilthey, means to make sense of the world, to understand.

EPISTEMOLOGY

Epistemologically, the constructivist takes a subjective position. The knower and the known are co-created during the inquiry. The researcher opts for a more personal, interactive mode of data collection. Constructivist epistemology has unique qualities that distinguish it from positivist epistemology. Wholeness, empathy, and subjectivity are assumptions that uniquely set apart positivists from constructivists.

Constructivist researchers strive to understand phenomena or a situation as a whole, looking for the unifying nature of particular settings. This holistic approach assumes that the whole is to be understood as a complex system that is greater than the sum of its parts. It also assumes that a description and understanding of a person's social environment or an organization's political context are essential for the overall understanding of what is observed.

The advantage of qualitative portrayals of holistic settings is that greater attention can be given to settings, interdependencies, complexities, idiosyncrasies, and context. Deutscher has argued that, despite the totality of our personal experiences as living, working human beings, researchers have mostly focused their studies solely on parts or fragments of wholes.[16]

We know that human behavior was rarely if ever directly influenced or explained by an isolated variable; we knew that it was impossible to assume that any of such variables were additive (with or without weighting); we knew that the complex mathematics of the interaction among any set of variables was incomprehensible to us. In effect, although we knew they did not exist, we defined them into being.[17]

It is no simple task to undertake holistic study, to search for wholes in a given situation. The challenge for the participant observer is to seek the essence of the life of the participant, to sum up and to find a central unifying principle. Understanding and seeking meaning in any situation requires a great deal of openness, empathy, and patience. Constructivist and interpretive studies become particularly useful where one needs to understand some special groups, particular problem, or unique situation in great depth and where one can identify and analyze complicated cases. The more a study aims at individualized outcomes, the greater the appropriateness of interpretive research methods.

METHODOLOGY

The interpretive/constructivist paradigm is hermeneutic and dialectic. Individual constructions are elicited and refined hermeneutically, and compared and contrasted dialectically, with the aim of generating one or a few constructions in which there is substantial consensus.[18] Multiple perspectives yield interpretations of meanings by participants and the researcher, who is considered to be the participant observer in the study.

Qualitative methods such as interviews, observations, document review, and analysis are predominant in a constructivist paradigm. These are applied accordingly to the assumption of the social construction of reality: that research can be conducted only by interaction between and among the researcher and participants.[19]

The methodological implication of having multiple realities is that research questions cannot be definitively established before the study begins; rather they will evolve and change as the study progresses. Qualitative methods are developmental and dynamic. A primary interest of a qualitative researcher is describing and understanding this

dynamic formulation of questions and its holistic effect on the participants who are providing ideas. In real-world conditions where settings, situations, and programs are subject to change and redirection,
qualitative inquiry replaces fixed treatment and controlled experi-
ment with a dynamic changing of and reflection on the data. Flexible
and dynamic research is not tied to a single treatment and predetermined goals or outcomes. It focuses on the actual process and operations over a period. The constructivist researcher sets out to understand the situation and describe it, making no attempt to manipulate,
control, or eliminate situational variables or any new development,
but accepting the complexity of a changing situation. The holistic,
dialectical assumptions of qualitative research methods allow the
researcher to understand multiple interrelationships among dimensions that emerge from the data without making prior assumptions or
specifying a hypothesis about the linear or correlative relationships.

THE DEBATE BETWEEN QUALITATIVE VS. QUANTITATIVE METHODS

Philosophers of science and methodologists have been engaged in a
long-standing epistemological and methodological debate about how
best to conduct research.[20] This debate has centered on the relative
value of two fundamentally different and competing inquiry paradigms that have been discussed above: positivism, which uses quantitative and experimental methods to *test* hypothetical deductive generalizations, versus interpretive/constructive inquiry, using qualitative and hermeneutic approaches to *understand* inductively and
holistically human experiences in context-specific settings.[21] This
debate covers differing ontologies and assumptions about the nature
of reality as discussed above. Yet I want to suggest that qualitative
inquiry is adopted by people who are comfortable with the idea of
generating multiple perspectives rather that the absolute truth.
Tolerance for ambiguity seems to be associated with comfort in dealing with perspectives rather than scientific facts and truths.

   In the following section, I shall focus on major issues of the debate,
such as subjectivity, objectivity, value-free, value-bound, and limitations of research statistical designs. First, however, I shall present a
general view of the issue.

Constructivists argue that one reason for moving away from scientific and a priori research is its inability to give a realistic and whole portrait of any educational or social situation. The conventional approach to research is limited in many ways, which makes it unable to encompass the complexity of the problems. Instead of loosening the grip over method so that reality unfolds naturally, more control is placed on the variables so as to observe, artificially, the reaction of the dependent variables.

Another argument that the constructivists state for adopting the alternative paradigm and research methods is that positivism does not have the capability of dealing with what Polyani called *tacit knowledge*, that is, intuitions, apprehensions, and feelings that are difficult to put into words. Polyani distinguished between propositional knowledge, that is, knowledge that can be stated in *language form*, and *tacit knowledge*.[22] Scientific inquiry limits itself to only a small part of propositional knowledge. However, the greater part of this knowledge and the whole of tacit knowledge remains untouched.

Another reason for moving away from conventional methods of inquiry is their quantitative, statistical approach to evaluation and the effect of such quantification on producing a fragmented body of knowledge. "Statistics represent a reductionist type of knowledge and is often viewed as the hard core of positivistic, empiricist science upholding objectivity and quantification as one and indivisible."[23] In addition, conventional methods of inquiry are equated with scientific approaches. The inappropriateness of this term 'scientific approach,' as applied to the use of statistics in social sciences, unfolds upon close examination of such a claim.

Science and scientific methods in the field of natural sciences are always associated with discoveries and inventions. In the social sciences, however, so-called scientific approaches aim at the verification of existing theories. The rigidity of the a priori design and the tight control of the situation being investigated hinders any opportunity for the unfolding of truth, not to mention discovery.

> One could say that statistics as a knowledge-seeking activity is not aimed at uncovering or exploring the essence of the things or their completeness but is an effort to dismantle the whole, to identify the

measurable parts that make up the whole, and then as a subordinate project perhaps put together a larger picture and information framework from the counted parts.[24]

Thus statistical methods for research and evaluation are erroneously called scientific, because true science aims at the discovery of truth. The limitation of statistics inherent in its orientation precludes such a claim. I refer to 'scientific methods' in this book as methods restricted to statistical designs.

OBJECTIVITY IN SCIENTIFIC INQUIRY

Objectivity is another myth associated with statistical designs. True science, I propose, would seek truth and leave the door open for the phenomena to unfold naturally without conditioning or controlling the situation; to interact naturally with the phenomena in hand, as in everyday communication. This approach is not acceptable within the present scientific mode of inquiry because researchers feel obliged to eliminate any subjective feelings toward the subjects being studied. Lack of empathy characterizes scientific methods of research and builds an artificial wall between the researcher and the participants, as Turner has noted:

> In its present form, empathy has nothing to do with science. There are no controls, no click, click, click, click. This is the thesis of Elias Canetti, 1981 Nobel laureate in literature (and doctor of chemistry)... An empathic person does not collect people, like data, to arrange them side by side in an orderly manner. He does not regard particular individuals as so many pesky non-recurrent events, to be wished away in favor of classifications and norms.
>
> Empathy is a gift to humankind, like rational thought, and some people are more empathetic than others.[25]

John Stewart Mill defined empathy as "The faculty by which one mind understands a mind different from itself, and throws itself into the feelings of that other mind."[26]

Curricula and educational practices generally have been criticized for the scientific, 'cold' language which is used by educators. Eisner said:

One is struck by the sober, humorless quality of so much of the writing in the field of curriculum and in educational research. The tendency towards what is believed to be scientific language has resulted in an emotionally eviscerated form of expression; any sense of the poetic or the passionate must be excised...Cool dispassionate objectivity has resulted in sterile, mechanistic language devoid of the playfulness and artistry that are essential to teaching and learning.[27]

SCIENTIFIC INQUIRY AS A VALUE-FREE ENTERPRISE

Another argument against scientific research is premised on the misconception that it is value-free, objective, and neutral. Yet Raskin argues:

> Without admitting it, colonizing knowledge relates to the elimination of alternate explanations, and the unwillingness to accept the interrelationships between the sort of science we do, how we do it, the questions we ask, and the sorts of 'proof' we require. At least since World War II scientists and technologists have integrated themselves with remarkable ease into the research and political programs of the powerful. They were expected to come up with those 'facts' that 'made things work.'[28]

The neutrality and freedom from value in scientific and educational research is a dangerous assumption that is fostered by the so-called scientific approach. Suppression of values, principles, and beliefs for the sake of being 'objective' cause severe damage to people and to humanity. It numbs the feelings and emotions and develops irresponsible individuals. Being aware of one's values and beliefs and re-examining them continually helps to direct people toward desirable ends.

Taking the stand of neutrality in value-laden situations of life indeed creates passive 'lukewarm' individuals who detach themselves from their research, their students, their participants, their society, and life in general. Most importantly, it causes severe damage to their moral consciousness.

Doctoral programs socialize students to believe that the most dependable procedure for obtaining knowledge is that of science and that respectable inquiry in education is scientific in character. To use other methods, to employ metaphor, analogy, simile, or other poetic devices, is to 'tell stories,' to lack rigor.[29]

SCIENTIFIC INQUIRY AS COLONIZING KNOWLEDGE

Scientifically oriented research is inappropriate for human sciences because it creates and develops a hierarchical way of thinking and acting. Gradually it affects the policy of educational institutes and the relationships between students and teachers, and creates a corrupt atmosphere of control and struggle. In fact, it develops a colonizing of knowledge and a colonizing of mentalities and personalities.

> Since the eighteenth century, the most powerful partner of colonizing knowledge has been scientific knowledge, the formulation of rules from empirical observation, and mathematics, which gives a modest level of understanding about the interaction of things in nature. I couple scientific knowledge with technical knowledge.[30]

The scientific, quantitative approach to research has developed a colonizing knowledge not only in the West, in Western institutions, but it has been introduced in and imposed on developing countries as well by United Nations development programs. Scientific knowledge has assumed the universality of social principles. Knowledge developed in the West under totally different social, cultural, economic, and political situations has been generalized and transferred to developing countries.

> They [Western politicians] assumed for the most part that the body of knowledge about social science learned in the universities of the West was pertinent to societies in general…It has been a shock to accept that the social processes we know to operate in the West are often absent or very subordinate to other social forces in the Third World.[31]

THE SUBJECTIVITY–OBJECTIVITY DILEMMA

The subjectivity–objectivity issue has been considered a major focal point of the methodological and epistemological debate. Subjectivity is often used to signify a form of contamination of a social and scientific inquiry.[32] To be subjective is to be 'biased,' allowing one's values to enter into and prejudice the outcome of one's research. Subjective data imply opinion rather than fact, intuition rather than logic, impression rather than confirmation.

The conventional means for controlling subjectivity and maintaining objectivity are the methods of quantitative social science: distance from the people being studied, operationalizing and statistical measurement, manipulation of isolated variables and experimental design. Yet the ways in which measures are constructed in educational and psychological tests and questionnaires are, in fact, no less open to the intrusion of the researcher's biases than making observations in the field or asking questions in interviews. "Numbers do not protect against biases, they merely disguise them. All statistical data are based on someone's definition of what to measure and how to measure it."[33] Scriven argues that quantitative methods are no more synonymous with objectivity than qualitative methods with subjectivity. Objectivity has been considered the strength of the scientific method. The primary methods for achieving objectivity in science have been conducting blind experiments and quantification. Data are gathered from objective texts that are, it is said, not dependent on human skill or perception. However, no one doubts that tests and questionnaires are designed by human beings and are subject to the intrusion of the researcher's biases. There are many cases of unconscious bias or even dishonesty on behalf of the researcher in the skillful manipulation of statistics to prove a hypothesis in which the researcher antecedently believes.

Qualitative rigor is concerned with the quality of observations made by the researcher. Therefore, instead of focusing on refining and re-refining the instrument and limiting it more to fit into the statistical design, emphasis must be put on refining the researcher since she or he is the instrument for gathering information and also the means for summarizing, classifying, and interpreting the data. Underlying assumptions of qualitative research emphasize the importance of human contact and intensive envelopment of the researcher in the respondents' lives.

Dialogue and dialectic are major concepts in the constructivist paradigm and qualitative methodology; therefore, the researcher has to find ways of being fair and objective without being detached and indifferent. Distance does not guarantee objectivity; it merely guarantees distance. Guba and Lincoln suggest 'fairness' as a substitute criterion.34 Patton suggests the concept of neutrality as a substitute for subjectivity: the neutral researcher enters the field with no axe to grind, no theory to prove, and no predetermined results to support.35 Rather, the researcher's commitment should be to the principles of the constructivist paradigm, its assumption of understanding wholeness, and the multiple realities of the situation under study.

NATURALISTIC SOLUTIONS
TO METHODOLOGICAL PROBLEMS

The credibility of qualitative research has always been questioned, since, according to positivists, such investigations violate all criteria of 'scientific research' such as objectivity, validity, reliability, replicability, and generalization. Issues of validity and reliability have been extensively discussed by qualitative methodologists.36 In the following section I shall present the criteria proposed by Guba and Lincoln to validate qualitative research methods.37 Theirs were among the early attempts to discuss the credibility of the alternative methods.

According to Guba and Lincoln, qualitative methods face accusations of being naive, sloppy, loose, subjective, untrustworthy, and lacking in rigor.38 In addition, questions have been raised regarding the internal and external validity, reliability, and objectivity of the naturalistic approach. The authors place these problems into three categories: bounding, focusing, and rigor. These three categories are now discussed in detail. See Table 3.1 for the assumptions of a scientific and a naturalistic paradigm.

First, "bounding problems relate to the task of establishing the boundaries of any inquiry as a whole."39 In traditional quantitative methods the boundaries are established before the evaluator starts her or his evaluation, and variables are controlled. In a qualitative inquiry there are no constraints, and questions emerge from the situation. It does not impose a priori constraints. The boundaries are established by the evaluator's client or sponsor and from the recycling common to all naturalistic inquiry. Guba and Lincoln state that "formulation of problems into a syllogistic format is useful because this format suggests several strategies for boundary designation."40

Second, because of the openness of qualitative research, data tend to expand and diverge and that is natural. However, the researcher should be aware of such divergence and be prepared for the convergent stage in the process. Focusing problems arise because, if outputs are not defined before the inquiry begins, then those outputs that are noted must be collected, analyzed, categorized, and interpreted after the fact. This situation gives rise to two subclasses of problems, namely, those of convergence and divergence.41

Third, meeting tests of rigor is the next methodological problem which faces qualitative inquiry. Problems of rigor arise from the inquirer's need to persuade other inquirers or audiences of the authenticity of the information provided and the interpretations that are drawn from it. Conventional scientific evaluation is based on positivism, a value-free approach, as assumption of singular reality, fragmentation, and controllable, generalizable assumptions. Its main concern is methodology and not the context nor the process of the study. It relies on criteria of rigor, namely, internal and external validity, reliability, and objectivity. Scientific inquiry has followed very closely the path of developmental psychology, which Bronfenbrenner criticized in these famous remarks:

> To corrupt a contemporary metaphor, we risk being caught between a *rock* and a *soft* place. The rock is *rigor*, and the soft place *relevance*...the emphasis on rigor has led to experiments that are elegantly designed but often limited in scope. This limitation derives from the fact that many of these experiments involve situations that are unfamiliar, artificial, and short-lived and that call for unusual settings that are difficult to generalize to other settings. From this perspective, it can be said that much of contemporary developmental psychology is the science of the strange behavior of children in strange situations with strange adults for the briefest possible periods of time.42

Questions of rigor are therefore very important in scientific inquiry to determine the credibility of the research. Constructive inquiry, however, is based on multiple constructed realities, interactions,

The Conventional and Naturalistic Belief Systems
[Table 3.1]

CONVENTIONAL POSTURE	NATURALISTIC POSTURE

ONTOLOGY

Realist
There exists a single reality independent of any observer's interest in it that operates according to immutable natural laws, many of which are causal in form. Truth is defined as facts isomorphic with reality.

Discretion
There exists multiple social constructed realities ungoverned by any natural laws. Truth is defined as the most informed and sophisticated construction(s) on which there is consensus among qualified critics.

EPISTEMOLOGY

Dualist, Objectivist
It is possible for an observer to exteriorize the reality studied, remaining detached from it and uninvolved with it.

Monist, Subjectivist
The inquirer and the inquirer-into are interlocked in such a way that the findings of the investigation are the literal creation of the inquiry process. (This assertion obliterates the ontology/epistemology disctinction).

METHODOLOGY

Interventionist
The context is stripped of its contaminating (confounding) influences so that the inquiry can converge on truth, explaining nature as it really is, leading to the capability to predict and control.

Hermeneutic
The context is construed as giving meaning and existence to the inquired-into; the methodology involves a dialectics of iteration, analysis, critique, reiteration, reanalysis, and so on; leading to the emergence of a joint (combined emic/etic) understanding of a case.

negotiation, holism, a value-bound approach and the contextual paradigm; in such an inquiry the main focus is the influence of context on the problem at hand (and vice versa). Therefore questions should be asked about the authenticity instead of the rigor of the evaluation. "Criteria developed from conventional axioms and rationally quite appropriate to conventional studies may be quite inappropriate and irrelevant to constructivist studies."43 Based on the two levels of qualitative research – method and paradigm – Lincoln and Guba suggest two sets of naturalistic criteria. One set caters to the demand for rigorous criteria, which is parallel to conventional criteria, that is 'trustworthiness' criteria. These criteria are intended to respond to four basic questions: *truth, value, applicability, consistency,* and *neutrality.* These can be answered from a constructivist point of view by using different terms. Thus in naturalistic terms, credibility, transferability, dependability, and confirmity will be used to substitute for internal validity, external validity, reliability, and objectivity in scientific evaluation.

FAIRNESS

Since constructivist inquiry is value-bound, and multiple realities and participation are important issues in naturalistic inquiry, "fairness may be defined as a balanced view that presents all constructions and the values that undergird them."44 Fairness can be achieved by (1) ascertaining and presenting different values and belief systems represented by conflict over issues; and by (2) negotiating the recommendations and subsequent action carried out with the participants.

ONTOLOGICAL AUTHENTICATION

If the aim of the study is to raise and unite consciousness, then ontological criteria can serve to determine to what extent the processes of evaluation and negotiation increase the appreciation and realization of participants in hidden political, social, economic, and educational issues which affect the contextual shaping of the present problem.

EDUCATIVE AUTHENTICATION

The educative criteria are concerned more with increased understanding of the 'whats' and 'whys' of various constructions that are rooted in different value systems of others. This deep understanding of issues adds to the complexity of the newly developed constructions of researchers and participants, both personally and professionally.

CATALYTIC AUTHENTICATION

Since the humanizing of education underlies the constructivist paradigm, the active inclusion of participants leads to their empowerment during evaluation. Therefore, according to the catalytic criterion, the researcher "involves all stakeholders from the start, honors their inputs that provides them with decision-making power in guiding the study,...[and] attempts to empower the powerless and give voice to the speechless."[45]

TACTICAL AUTHENTICITY

This criterion is concerned with whether the study is empowering or impoverishing, and to whom, Therefore, by collaborative negotiation, participants gain some practice and understanding of various and conflicting constructions. Thus the participants are no longer 'subjects' to be controlled and manipulated by the researcher or powerful groups.

CHAPTER FOUR

Critical Reflection on Existing Paradigms

Having presented both positivist and constructivist paradigms, I want to argue at this point that not all existing paradigms in social sciences in the West are suitable for producing holistic Islamic knowledge that is appropriate for the development of Muslim societies for the following reasons:

- All existing paradigms, conventional and alternative, are fragmented and have 'either/or' qualities; therefore, they cannot advance wholeness.
- Existing paradigms in social sciences deal with all issues at one level only, that is to say, they do not consider transcendent qualities to deal with the 'unseen and hereafter.'
- The positivist paradigm is a closed and fragmented system that does not allow for the natural flow of information.
- The constructivist/interpretive paradigm is fragile and can be easily abused or misused because of its openness and relativity. Realities are constructed and multiple. There does not exist an Absolute Reality according to the constructivist paradigm.

Since the main concern of this book is epistemology, education, and knowledge production from an Islamic perspective, I should like to reflect on positivism/interpretivism from a teaching/learning perspective. Teaching and learning have always been among the most important concepts in Islam. The word knowledge (ʿilm) is repeated in the Qur'an many times. Learning and acquiring knowledge are considered a form of worship (ʿibādah). Learning may be defined as the making of a new or revised interpretation of the meaning of an experience. It guides subsequent understanding, appreciation, and action. What we perceive or fail to perceive and what we learn or fail to learn are strongly influenced by our value system, which is integrated in our personality and our thinking, as well as our frame of reference. It is our belief system that structures the way in which we perceive, interpret, and understand our experiences. To make meaning is to make sense of an experience. When we use our interpretation to guide decision-making or action, then making meaning becomes learning. Learning can be pleasant or unpleasant, and that depends on the material being taught and the methods used to convey that teaching.

In the present time most studies and theories have emerged from research based on the positivist or interpretivist paradigm. In positivism, most theories of the education of sociology and psychology are fragmented, unidimensional, unconnected, and meaningless. They are based on experimental statistical designs. So the learner either acquires those theories of learning as they are and builds her or his knowledge accordingly with all the shortcomings of these theories, or, on rare occasions, develops a reflective and critical view, and is able to analyze them and modify them where possible, or reject them outright.

However, in the case of interpretivism, although the theories produced are more meaningful and more integrated, they are limited from a transcendental point of view. The interpretive/constructivist paradigm is unable to encompass life in its wholeness. It is based on the belief system that "realities are ungoverned by any natural laws and truth is defined as the most informed and sophisticated constructions on which there is consensus among qualified critics."[1] So reality, according to this view, is marginalized and fragmented to what is seen, felt, and perceived by people. There does not exist a 'given' reality which one strives to understand and attain. Reality from an Islamic perspective has a transcendental and metaphysical dimension. Multiplicity, which is a major component in constructivism, is only a manifestation of the ultimate truth from an Islamic perspective, which has yet to be sought and understood by human beings. This dimension is ignored by constructivists.

> The Principle is Reality in contrast to all that appears as real but which is not reality in the ultimate sense. The Principle is the Absolute compared to which all is relative. It is infinite while all is finite. The

Principle is One and unique while manifestation is multiplicity...It is the Essence to which all things are juxtaposed as form.[2]

Therefore, reality from an Islamic perspective is physical and metaphysical. At the physical level reality can be constructed by the people taking part in any study, but even that reality is guided by the Divine Principle and the absolute truth. Positivism, on the other hand, has its shortcomings, which have been explained in detail in earlier chapters. Reality from the positivist is singular, unidimensional, and independent of any observer's interest. "Reality exists 'out there' and is driven by immutable natural laws and mechanisms. Knowledge of these entities, laws and mechanics is conventionally summarized in the form of time and context-free generalizations."[3]

Despite the great differences in their perspective, reality in both paradigms are limited to the physical level. Denial of the Absolute, the metaphysical, and the sacred knowledge characterizes both paradigms and hence makes them both unable to encompass the complexity of the Islamic perspective of reality and its multiple dimensions of the physical and the metaphysical.

So as a Muslim researcher, I find myself trapped in the rigidity of positivism and the looseness of constructivism. When a paradigm is rooted in religion, as is the Islamic paradigm, there are religious laws that regulate life at every level, including relativity in daily life. Those laws are intended to keep individuals on the right path (al ṣirāt al-mustaqīm).

A holistic perspective would encompass both the objective world, which is absolute, permanent, fixed, and metaphysical, and the subjective world, which is relative, temporary, flexible, and material. A person with such a perspective will agree that neither positivism nor interpretivism is suitable as a paradigm and belief system. As a Muslim educator, I believe that neither of the paradigms is appropriate for producing knowledge that is relevant to Islamic society and Muslim communities around the world. As explained earlier in Chapter 1, children are exposed to religion and spirituality from an early age: every activity has some religious connotation and is done according to the Sharī'ah (Islamic law) – from birth to death. So most of our experiences are rooted in the Islamic paradigm. Religion in Islam is a way of life; it is not just a ritual performed on Fridays in mosques. Our daily activities are colored with Islamic values, so learning, making meaning, and interpreting new situations are all done in an Islamic frame of reference.

Much of what we humans learn requires new interpretations that enable us to elaborate, further differentiate, and reinforce our long-established frames of references or create new meaning schemes. Perhaps even more important for scholars and graduate students than elaborating established meaning schemes is reflection on what has been learnt to determine whether it is justified under present circumstances or in the light of old and new paradigms. All existing paradigms are fragmented in one way or another. They are either objective like positivism or subjective like interpretivism, but their common characteristic is that they are 'this worldly.' In other words, they both deal with life as if it starts here in this world and ends here too; they assume that we are here to live, enjoy and destroy all God's blessings, and then die, and that is the end of human beings and creation. It is important to clarify here that the discussion is at paradigm level and that includes ontology and epistemology, and is not restricted to methodology alone. The shortcoming is not so much in the constructivist methods as in the constructivist paradigm. The constructivist paradigm is relative and temporal; those assumptions cannot accommodate transcendent and metaphysical, fixed and permanent principles of the unseen and the hereafter.

Such a paradigm definitely cannot encompass the wholeness of the Islamic belief system, which is rooted in the concept of 'this world' and 'the hereafter' (al-dunyā wa al-ākhira): these two words are repeated in the Divine Book many times to reflect the centrality of this concept in Islam. Thus, an Islamic paradigm and methodology are needed for Islamic societies, and Muslim scholars should seek to produce knowledge that is congruent with the Islamic belief system and rooted in the Divine Book of Islam. The Islamic paradigm has existed since the revelation of the Qur'an, and Islamic civilization with its richness and contribution to all branches of knowledge – mathematics, medicine, cosmology, geography, astronomy, and other sciences – is witness to the success of such a paradigm.

The Islamic revelation, like all major manifestations of the Divine Logos, not only produced a religion in the sense of an ethical and social code, but also transformed a segment of the cosmos and the minds of those who have lived within that cosmic sector. The phenomenon which formed the subject matter of the Islamic sciences as well as the mind of the men who studied the phenomenon has always been determined by a particular spiritual 'style' and transformed by a special type of grace (*barakah*) issuing directly from the Qur'an revelation.4

Therefore, wholeness and holiness are characteristics of Islamic science, Islamic knowledge, and Islamic civilization. Islamic epistemology is rooted in spirituality and holiness. What makes Islamic science unique is the combination of the humanistic dimension and the divine dimension; the material and the sacred. Islamic science, fourteen centuries ago, provided humanity with a scientific, humanistic, spiritual base for the development and advancement of knowledge. Yet, Western societies have entrusted their knowledge, their lives, and their souls to human minds, which are limited and unable to encompass the complexity of the cosmos and the nature of humankind. The destruction of nature, society, and human beings is a witness of such limitations.

Academics and intellectuals have been struggling with issues of ethics and morality in the academic arena for decades. Debates about facts and values, objectivity and subjectivity, religion and science were invading universities even more than before. Scientists and philosophers were going from one extreme to the other, from objectivity to subjectivity and back. Contradictions and confusion were distorting people's clarity of vision and common sense. Both Western and Eastern scholars were confused and overreacting to each other's propositions. The latest and strongest reaction that I have come across is what is called by Banaie and Haque the 'equegeneric principle.'5 In their book they claim to have refuted all possible ideas and concepts of the methods of finding the truth. The writers reject all 'isms': positivism, relativism, and mysticism. The secular worldview as well as the religious worldview are rejected as unsuitable means for establishing a value system for society:

> The two commonly used sources of morality are religion and secularism (conventional systems), both of which are problematic for none of them is purely subservient to discovered facts. In the case of religious values, what constitutes as religion to begin with? We must consider that theology is not a universal science like biology, for any idiot can grab a piece of paper and pen and write what he would claim to be divine revelation. If the notion of 'religion' is not universal, consequently, the values derived from 'religion' cannot possibly be universal.[6]

Then they proceed to refute secularism and the permanent values established by such a system. They reject all the philosophical, historical, social, scientific, and religious concepts under the sun and establish their own vocabulary for an old concept. 'Natural principles' or 'natural laws' have replaced 'equegeneric' because, according to the authors, the concept of 'natural law' has been misused.

Rationality, solid objectivity, facts, cause and effect are the focus of the 'equegeneric principle.' We are back to square one of unidimensionality and reductionism. The two authors reject all 'isms' just to create their own 'ism.' They assert that:

> The internal faculty – must always objectively interact with the external reality – the universe. Our methodology must be in absolute congruity with the universe of cause and effect, and furthermore, it ought to be consistent within itself.[7]

The authors have forgotten that we as human beings are limited, and that we make meaning out of our own daily simple and complex experiences and that we have to discipline our minds and souls as we understand the world around us. Moreover, they forget that human beings are multidimensional in their faculties and that we have to use different inquiry methods to understand intellectual and spiritual experiences. We use our minds to understand certain things, yet we use our hearts and our souls to understand and make sense of other issues.

Therefore, any methodology used by Muslim scholars ought to be a holistic method in the true sense of wholeness. Islam considers knowledge in its totality and these two perspectives have been illustrated by John Sahadat .

First, as it pertains to the phenomenal world and the scientific method of investigation; second, as it pertains to the metaphenomenal (that is, the Divine and His Revelation to humanity) and the Islamic method of acceptance based on faith and verification, devotion and experience. Knowledge is not only 'cosmoanthropocentric' as is science, but also 'cosmotheathropocentric,' which is inclusive of the three fundamental frames of reference: the cosmos, God, and humankind. This is the tridimensional foundation of Islamic education.

Western education, owing to its limitations, is incapable of capturing the richness and complexity of human beings, God, and the cosmos. So instead of understanding natural phenomena as a whole with all their dimensions, positivists and relativists have cut the phenomena into slices and studied each slice separately, assuming that when the parts are put together, they will have the complete picture. By doing so, they have neglected the relationship between the parts, as if each part of the phenomena lived in isolation from and had no interaction with the other parts.

The damage that positivism has done to the structure of Western civilization is irrecoverable, mainly because the damage is in the roots of human consciousness. When a person adopts positivism as a philosophy or as an academic base for her/his intellectual activities and exercises, that base becomes a belief system. That belief system rules all her or his daily activities as well as relationships at home and at work. The rigid 'scientific' reductionist training colors all of that person's life and activity. When that scientist starts studying any phenomena, she or he starts applying what was learned in methodology courses. She or he starts *manipulating* the phenomena, *controlling* the variables, *separating* the phenomena from the environment and then cuts the complex system into pieces so as to be able to control it and study it thoroughly. Most importantly, positivists separate themselves from the phenomena under study so as to maintain *objectivity*. Once a raw mind is trained in these scientific rituals, it will treat everything and everybody in the same way. After so many years of such rigorous scientific training, we, as researchers, can vividly see the damage that it has done to the Western mind.[8]

III

ISLAMIC KNOWLEDGE

CHAPTER FIVE

The Islamic Worldview: The One and the Many

> The Islamic worldview is religious, rational and philosophical, it is all encompassing and leads to oneness.
>
> Islam's ultimate purpose is to reveal the Unity of the Divine Principle and to integrate the world of multiplicity in the light of that Unity. Spirituality in Islam is inseparable from the awareness of the One, of Allah, and a life lived according to His Will.
>
> The Principle of Unity (*tawḥīd*) lies at the heart of the Islamic message and determines Islamic spirituality in all its multifarious dimensions and forms. Spirituality is *tawḥīd* and the degree of spiritual attainment achieved by any human being is none other than the degree of his or her realization of *tawḥīd*.[1]

In this chapter I should like to shed some light on the Islamic worldview to help the reader to see the sharp distinction between Western secular philosophy and Islamic religious philosophy. Islamic philosophy is deeply rooted in religious and theological teachings. The focus of Islamic religion, philosophy, and epistemology is on the development of the human being. Purification of the soul by the moral and ethical teachings of the Qur'an and sharpening of the mind by reasoning and reflection on God's creation, the universe, and the self are the ultimate goals of Islamic teachings and practice.

> Do they never, never ponder among themselves? Truly Allah has not created the heavens and the earth and all that is in between except with a clear design and a definite plan in time. (The Qur'an, 30:8)

The purpose of developing the inner power of human beings by reinforcing good and eradicating evil is prescribed in Islam because human beings are considered to hold a high position in God's creation. And the purpose of humankind on earth is to reach the highest level of perfection from knowledge of the self, the universe, and God – Who is the Ultimate Truth – and by actions which should be rooted in morality and ethics. Humankind holds the highest and most noble position on earth. When God created Adam, He asked the angels to prostrate themselves before him to make him aware of his position so that he should not degrade himself.

> When your Lord said to the angels, "I am creating a man of clay. So when I have shaped him, and breathed My Spirit into him, fall down prostrating before him." So the angels prostrated themselves all together. (The Qur'an, 38:71-73)

It is important here to make a distinction between Islam, which is the essence, and Muslims or Muslim societies, which are the actual practice – and sometimes in sharp contrast to the essence of Islam. Al-Fārūqī states:

> In the writings of many authors Islam is confused with the Muslims. Such authors understand the legacy of thought, action, and expression by Muslims as constitutive of Islam itself…Claiming to be the perfect and primordial religion of God. Islam cannot be identified with Muslims' history. It is the ideal to which all Muslims strive and by which they would and should be defined. Hence, true objectivity demands that Islam be distinguished from Muslim history and instead be regarded as its essence, its criterion and its measure.[2]

Perfection, from an Islamic point of view, is associated with knowledge and action. This knowledge, however, is not for its own sake. It is mainly the right path for understanding the self, the universe, and ultimately God, and for bringing one close to Him. As Ibn Sīnā said, the human soul is continually learning to join the 'active intellect.' The Qur'an is based on the ultimate truth of God's knowledge, and the first verse which was revealed to the Prophet says:

> Read: In the name of your Lord Who created man from a blood clot.
> Read: For your Lord is the Most Beneficent, Who taught by the pen.
> He taught man that which he knew not. (The Qur'an, 96:1-5)

Muslim scholars and philosophers in the early period of Islam were believers in God, and in their search for truth they made every effort to understand His words in the Sacred Text. They were true Muslims, who submitted to the truth of God's words and humbled their powerful minds and their wise souls to the words of God so as to quench their thirst from the purest source of knowledge.

Muslim countries have, for many years, suffered degeneration and disintegration of their knowledge and action. Lack of harmony, continual inconsistency and distortion have characterized Muslim societies. Yet these societies, despite modernization and Westernization, are still religious and traditional. The majority of Muslims still believe in God, the Prophets, the Sacred Text, the angels, the Day of Judgment, and the hereafter. In most Muslim countries nowadays, one can notice the split and discord between the political and economic systems and the social system. It is the struggle between the center and the periphery. The conflict is between the government, the educated elite, and financially powerful people, and the rest of society, the ordinary people.

Most educational, social and economic systems, on the one hand, have been based on a Western, secular worldview, resulting in the imposition of Western education and technology with all the culture that comes with them. The rest of society, on the other hand, still has some resemblance to early Muslim societies. Communities, and family life based on legal and normal marriages, are still the foundation of Muslim societies. Respect for elderly people, parents, and teachers is still the spirit in those societies. Spirituality, piety, temperance, modesty, chastity, and self-sacrifice have not vanished completely.

The education system in Muslim societies is imported and imposed from outside. This is especially true of higher education, which is a complete transplantation of a Western system, with all its materialistic and secular characteristics, into the body of Islamic societies with all their religious, spiritual, and traditional identity. The mismatch between the Islamic, religious foundation of society and the secular, modern, Westernized education system, which is built on that foundation, will no doubt cause fractures and cracks in that building. Eventually it will collapse, causing severe damage which will last for a long time before that society starts to recover.

Because Islam's worldview upholds a single primordial nature, it favors both a single ideology and a single culture. Only a human ideology, not a corporate ideology, a unitive ideology, not one based on the division, and fragmentation of man, primordial ideology, not a profit-oriented one, can rest on human values and be human in its essence.[3]

The Islamic worldview is not purely religious. The uniqueness of Islam is in this profound and challenging belief in both the material and the religious worlds: Muslims should live this life and enjoy God's given gifts in moderation, yet believe in the hereafter and consider this life a purposeful journey which should be made with knowledge and filled with good deeds. The knowledge and action that Muslims spend their entire lives cultivating are to take them higher on the ladder of humanity and perfection and bring them closer to God and therefore to eternal life.

This blend of the two extremes is what Islam is about: the combination of a religious, contemplative life and a material, practical, worldly life. Yet the Western thinker, Habermas, for reasons unknown – to me at least – cannot incorporate this combination into his conceptional scheme. He has divided worldviews between the East and the West, and created a chart based solely on that division (see Table 5.1). On the one hand he describes the Judaic and Christian attitudes toward the world as "Active: Asceticism or Vita Activa, Ascetic turning towards the world, and Mastery of the world."[4] On the other hand, he describes the Confucian and Hindu worldviews as "Passive: Mysticism or the Vita Contemplativa, Flight from the world, Mystical turning away from the world."[5] Islam, one of the greatest religions in the world, is entirely excluded from the above discussion by Habermas! Islam, indeed, falls between these two extremes and challenges its followers to keep the balance between the active and the passive to create a balanced, harmonious way of living and thinking.

The Islamic worldview urges its followers to unify knowledge and action to create a synthesis of unitive knowledge and realize the Islamic worldview of *tawḥīd*. To synthesize opposites and contradictions, one needs a dialectical thinking, in my view, to be able to attain unity and *tawḥīd*.

Attitudes Towards the World[6]
[Table 5.1]

Ways of Seeking Salvation or of Securing the World	Active Asceticism or the Vita Activa	Passive Mysticism or the Vita Contemplativa
Evaluation of the World as a Whole		
Rejection of the World	Mastery of the World	Flight from the World (Hinduism)
Affirmation of the World	Adjustment to the Word (Confucianism)	

The following sections deal with (1) the Islamic worldview; (2) Islamic epistemology; and (3) al-Ghazālī's theory of knowledge and values (ethics).

THE ISLAMIC WORLDVIEW OF *TAWḤĪD*

The Islamic worldview, as stated by Mutahhari, is religious, philosophical, and rational. It is a worldview of *tawḥīd* or monism. This worldview regards God as the absolute reality and the source of being. *Tawḥīd* is the essence of Islam, it is the act of affirming God to be the One, Absolute, Eternal, and Transcendental Creator.

> As the affirmation of the absolute unity of God, *tawḥīd* is the affirmation of the unity of truth. For God, in Islam, is the truth. His unity is the unity of the sources of truth. God is the creator of nature whence man derives his knowledge. The object of knowledge are [is] the patterns of nature which are the work of God. Certainly God knows them since He is their author, and equally certainly He is the source of revelation. He gives man of His knowledge; and His knowledge is absolute and universal...God is perfect and omniscient. He makes no mistakes. Otherwise, He would not be the transcendent God of Islam.[7]

Since *tawḥīd* is the essence of Islam, it will be discussed in detail, especially as the concept runs through this book as a river runs through the valleys and plains and brings life to the lands nearby. The 'dialectics of *tawḥīd*' is the basis of this book, uniting ideas and giving life to them. The concept of the 'dialectics of *tawḥīd*' – its differing and apparently opposed manifestations – might cause unease in some readers because of the paradoxical meaning that it carries. *Tawḥīd* means oneness and unity, whereas dialectics means opposing ideas and conflict. However, for me it is another way of understanding the 'One and the many.' Dialectics is embedded in *tawḥīd* naturally, as will be explained below. *Tawḥīd* is discussed by Muslim scholars on two levels: theoretical and practical. From a theoretical point of view Muslim scholars believe in God as the One and Absolute Being and the only source of truth and knowledge. According to Ibn Sīnā, because an actual infinite is deemed impossible,

> this chain [of being] as a whole must terminate in a being that is holy, simple and one, whose essence is its very existence, and therefore, is self-sufficient and not in need of something else to give it existence. Because its existence is not contingent on or necessitated by something else but is necessary and eternal in itself, it satisfies the condition of being the necessitating cause of the entire chain that constitutes the eternal world of contingent existing things.[8]

From a practical point of view, however, Muslims are obliged to follow the dialectical path of *tawḥīd* not only as the essence of their belief, but also to bring unity and harmony to their lives and thoughts. Reality is of two generic kinds: absolute and relative, spiritual and material, worldly and other worldly, stable and mutable, eternal and temporary. Muslims, therefore, use the concept of the dialectics of *tawḥīd* to unify these apparently contradictory concepts. From an Islamic standpoint, these concepts are complementary and not contradictory. That is why true Muslims do not believe in either–or schools of thought. Realities are twofold: a simple and self-evident example is humankind. A human being has a body, mind, and soul. To be able to function properly, one aspect should not be developed at the expense of the others. The duty of humankind is to maintain the balance so that each part complements the others instead of being in conflict with them. Unifying or maintaining the balance between the extremes is not an easy task. Life is full of irony and paradoxes in which one must make decisions yet keep the inward and outward balance of the self. "Since the divine pattern is the norm that reality ought to actualize, the analysis of what is should never lose sight of what *ought to be*."9

On the surface this sounds like another version of Hegel's dialectical idealism or Marx's dialectical realism. Sharif, in an attempt to clarify the differences from an Islamic point of view, presents the following hypothesis: Hegelian ideas and Marxist realities are not of opposite natures; they are in conflict.10 They are mutually warring ideas or warring realities. In the case of Marx's classes, they are separated by hostility and hatred.

> In the movement of history [according to the Islamic worldview] *real* selves are attracted by *ideals* and then in realizing them, are synthesized with them. This movement is dialectical but it is totally different from the Hegelian or Marxist dialectic. Their thesis and anti-thesis are struggling against each other. Here, one is struggling not 'against' but 'for' the other...The dialectic of human society, according to this formula is not a struggle of warring classes or warring nations but a struggle against limitations to realize goals and ideas which goals and ideals are willed and loved rather than fought against.11

By adopting and practicing *tawḥīd* as a worldview, a Muslim is trained to be one whole integrated self, which has an ultimate aim, that of reaching the highest level of perfection through the struggle for ideal knowledge and action. That is ultimate happiness, according to al-Ghazālī. *Tawḥīd* and the concept of unity save humankind from a continual struggle against ideals, from having a split society, and a split personality that thinks, speaks, and acts in a contradictory way.

This unity should not stop at the individual level but extend to society. Community life and the family structure are the foundation of Islamic societies. If the dialectics of *tawḥīd* and unity underlies the relationships in these communities, people with different philosophies in life learn, not necessarily without difficulty, how to bring their differences together and harmonize in society. Most importantly, they learn how to be tolerant and accept one another's differences. This does not mean conformity to one ideology or another.

For every one of you, We appointed a law and a way, and if Allah had pleased, He would have made you a single people, but that He might try you in what He gave you, therefore, strive with one another to hasten to virtuous deeds. To Allah will all return, so He will inform you of that wherein you differed. (The Qur'an, 5:48)

Tawḥīd is a principle that encourages people to be open-minded and tolerant of opposing points of view by discussing differences and trying to choose the one view which is closer to the ultimate truth, that is, God's words, or the one which does not deviate from the right path. "This is a dialectic of love rather than of hatred. It leads individuals, masses, classes, nations, and civilizations from lower to higher and from higher to yet higher reaches of achievement."[12]

So the dialectics which is embedded in *tawḥīd* elevates human beings from the material to the spiritual life through knowledge and action. Knowledge of the self, the universe, and God leads to the realization of the ultimate truth and that the Author of this creation is the Ultimate Truth. This encourages true believers to strive for the ideal and to realize that the real is only a means for rising above their desires and ascending toward the true light, like the sunflower that directs its movements to face the sun, or any plant that struggles toward the light if it is kept in the dark.

Man occupies a position midway between animals and angels; and his distinguishing quality is knowledge. He can either rise to the level of the angels with the help of knowledge, or fall to the level of the animals by letting his anger and lust dominate him. It is, therefore, knowledge which helps the growth of the divine element in him and makes possible the realization of the ideal.[13]

Therefore, the concept of *tawḥīd* indicates to Muslims the necessity for a continual search for the truth, to balance the dialectics of the real and the ideal, and to penetrate the unseen and the invisible to be able to find and judge for themselves the validity of that truth. *Tawḥīd* is a divine principle for free thinking, that type of thinking which is based on a dialectics between apparently opposing ideas, and gives everybody the opportunity to express his or her opinion. This expression of opinion must be based on an investigation for the truth and on knowledge. So free speech and the free choice of one philosophy over another are rooted in knowledge and actual realization of facts, not in public opinion and distorted images injected by the media, which are controlled by a group of politicians and businessmen who want to direct the whole world.

Tawḥīd is the essence of Islam, and its characteristics of unity, harmony, and oneness are what make Islam unique, comprehensive, and all-encompassing. It is this sense of mystery that makes it simple and understandable for ordinary people, and yet complex and difficult for great scholars and philosophers, who spend all their lives in pursuit of the truth in an attempt to discover the mysteries of the Qur'an. It is this blend of simplicity and complexity, of the absolute and the relative, the stable and the mutable, the eternal and the temporal, the soul and the body, good and evil, that challenges humankind and urges it to search for the truth. The challenge for Muslims, therefore, is, on the one hand, to believe in the Oneness of God among all the contradictory phenomena, that He is the only source of being and truth, and that His Knowledge is all-encompassing. On the other hand, Muslims are challenged to live and think in a unifying harmonious way among all of the controversies and apparently contradictory phenomena; to be able to realize the ideal and the truth, and strive for that truth through knowledge of the self, the universe, and action manifested in good deeds to serve society and humankind in general. It is by adopting the Islamic worldview of *tawḥīd* that Muslims can reach this level of perfection.

DEVELOPMENT FROM AN ISLAMIC PERSPECTIVE

The concept of social development for Islam is entirely different from the current Western idea of development. The ultimate goal in most Western, secular development projects that are designed and exported to Islamic countries is material and economic gain. In Islam such a goal is only the initial stage of the long journey of human and social development. Material development represents one stage in the transcendence to higher stages. Since human beings are regarded as a microcosm and society as a macrocosm, this issue might be better understood if development is discussed, first at the human level, and then transferred to the societal level. A comparison with developmental psychology and theories of child and adult development shows that almost all of these theories start with the concrete material state and move to the abstract and unknown stage. This upward movement is an innate desire in the whole of creation to aim for perfection. The spiral movement of perfection from the physical to the spiritual is a major concern in development theories.

Stages of development are related instrinsically to ways of thinking. When the aims of development start and end at the material level, as is true of the imported secular models, they reflect the thinking level of their designers. They also reflect the level of devotion and thinking in the Islamic societies that have agreed to implement proudly these alien secular models that have defaced Islamic identity. Developing the dialectics of *tawḥīd* is the highest stage of development in Islam. Without dialectical thinking, Muslims cannot accept the challenge of wholeness. To harmonize two opposites in one whole is not an easy task. But high standards, a better quality of life, education, and work are all difficult tasks. They are all challenging. The either–or frame of mind may make life easier, but it is one-dimensional. Conflict, differences, and contradictions belong only to the material or spiritual world, considered separately. Realizing the difficulty of the task, Islam proposes the dialectics of *tawḥīd* as a path to attain and fulfill the Divine Will for perfection.

THE MIND FROM AN ISLAMIC PERSPECTIVE

An important element in the transition of the physical to the spiritual is the mind. Through the mind, humans evolve to reach higher stages of their beings – their souls. It is mind and thought that separate humans from nonhumans. According to Qur'anic teachings, the human is placed in a hierarchy between angels and animals. Angels are distinguished by their pure intellect and they represent the spiritual world for which humans should strive; animals represent the material world from which humans should gradually move during their journey of development. The challenge for human beings, in Islam, is that they possess a mind to think and decide for themselves whether they want to ascend to higher levels or descend to lower levels. Neither angels nor animals possess both qualities: neither challenge nor struggle is experienced in their lives. Animals follow their animal desires naturally, and angels follow their pure intellect and spiritual desire to worship God day and night. But human beings have accepted the challenge that the universe refused to accept.

> We [God] had offered the Trust [of divine responsibilities] to the heavens, the earth, the mountains, but they refrained from bearing the burden and were frightened of it; but man took it on himself. He is a self-deluded simpleton. (The Qur'an, 33:72)

Therefore, for Islam, development has an entirely different goal and different dimensions. Any development in Islamic societies should focus on creating human beings as integrated wholes – body, mind, and soul. Human beings are the foundation and building blocks in any society. If they are fragmented and split, any construction on that foundation will collapse. So what integrates the body and the soul is the mind. For this reason, thinking and reflection in the Islamic school of thought hold the highest position. It is by thinking and reflection on the creation of the universe that one ascends from the concrete to the abstract, the temporary to the eternal, the relative to the absolute, the material to the spiritual, from the real – the 'is' – to the ideal of the 'ought to be.' So the path to human development, according to the Qur'anic school, is through knowledge.

Islam lays the maximum emphasis on improving the faculty of thinking in God's universe. Inequality among human beings, from the Islamic perspective, can be justified, if at all, on the basis of the differences of knowledge among them. It may be noted that after the word 'Allah,' 'knowledge' is the second most-repeated word in the Holy Qur'an.[14]

Ibn Khaldūn, the fourteenth-century Muslim scholar, in his encyclopedic work *al-Muqaddimah*, describes in detail the effect of excessive material development and how it disintegrates the human psyche and civilizations. At the very base of Ibn Khaldūn's paradigm of civilization's rise and fall stands his vision of human nature, especially that of the dialectic type: a potentially conflictual coexistence of human and animalistic inclinations. Daoudi summarizes Ibn Khaldūn's approach as follows:

On the one hand, the distinct human predispositions, particularly thinking and reasoning, enable man to build and continuously transform human civilization for the better.

On the other, Ibn Khaldūn considers the domination of Man's behavior by animalistic materialistic forces as a major obstacle in the theory to the most fundamental foundations of human civilization and at the same time as destructive factors, in practice, to the development of those foundations themselves. Thus for the author of the *Muqaddimah* the very rise of Arab Muslim civilization seems to have been contingent on certain conditions which existed among the earlier founders/Bedouins of the empire. Ibn Khaldun describes Bedouins as people whose worldly affairs do not go beyond basic necessities. Their nature is preserved free from distorted habits. They are people who accept quickly religious truths and right guidance. Cooperation is strong among them because of the prevailing spirit of *Al-Assabia* (group feeling).[15]

Therefore, according to Ibn Khaldūn, excessive materialistic development leads to the inevitable corruption and fall of societies and individuals. For Islam, materialistic fulfillment should be practiced in moderation to satisfy the basic needs of human beings and enable them to continue their journey of transformation to higher levels. The corruption of most Islamic countries and individual Muslims is due partly to the modernization programs launched in Islamic societies. Economic development and materialistic growth are the main features of these programs. The fourteenth-century ideas of Ibn Khaldūn are strikingly relevant:

> In this type of culture the typical individual has become profoundly materialistic and luxury-oriented. His thinking and reasoning [the distinct human traits according to Ibn Khaldūn] are more and more preoccupied with the satisfaction of his own pressing materialistic [animalistic] greed. With the spread of this tendency in all social classes and categories of population, a growing individualistic egoism is bound to be born. And with it society/civilization's social solidarity is seriously undermined.[16]

A sharp contrast exists between the secular, materially oriented worldview and the religious Islamic worldview. According to Islam,

life does not end in this world. It is only the material body that perishes; the spirit continues its journey in the other world. It is in the
other world that the actions and knowledge of human beings are
judged and evaluated. Life is a purposeful journey whose ultimate
goal is the unity of God's knowledge. So, the ultimate goal is the
realization of the essence of existence through knowledge of the self
that leads to realizing the essence in God's knowledge, which is the
Ultimate Truth. To reach that goal, people first have to realize the
essence of their being.

From an Islamic perspective, perfection corresponds to an awareness
of the soul, which is situated at the center of each person. Realizing
that there is a higher significance to life than the mere satisfaction of
basic material needs, individuals are motivated to aim for that higher
goal. When spirituality becomes the center of one's being and the
material the periphery, individuals evolve gradually and dialectically
and move away from the multiplicity of the worldly to the unity of the
Divine Principle. Self-awareness in all religions is associated with the
knowledge of the soul. However, the soul is a mysterious phenomenon that does not yield its secrets, even to the ancient wisdom.

The journey starts from the inner self to reach the Ultimate, the
One. If the self's transformation can be described in terms of a journey
from imperfection to perfection, or from forgetfulness to remembrance and mindfulness, it can also be understood as a passage from
dispersion to unity. The self is a single reality with multiple faculties
and dimensions. The oneness lies in the direction of the divine/human
spirit, while its multiplicity pertains to the body with its many parts
and functions.

> Here the geometrical image is that of a point at the center of a circle,
> the more the self turns towards its own center or source, the spirit, the
> more it becomes integrated and whole. But the more it leads towards
> the circumference, the body and the world, the more it becomes
> dispersed. 'Perfection' or full 'remembrance' then corresponds to awa
> reness situated at the center of the circle. The circumference no lon
> ger attracts the self, thereby drawing it into dispersion, but instead

represents the self's active and conscious self-manifestation within the bounds of its own perfected nature.[17]

Purification of the soul is another challenge for Muslims that attracts them toward the inner being, even more so as to discover and unfold the secrets of the soul. The Sufi, Jalāl al-Dīn Rūmī, states:

> The Prophet connected knowledge of God to knowledge of the soul and made the former conditional upon the latter when he said, "He who knows his soul knows his Lord." This indicates that no created being can know the soul in all its attributes or attain to the inmost core of its knowledge, any more than knowledge of God's inmost core can be attained.[18]

Self-awareness, knowledge of the soul, and perfection are interconnected and lead to the realization of the Unity of the Divine Principle. In the processes of perfection, the soul is torn between worldly and other-worldly states. The more the soul resists the temptation to satisfy materialistic desires, the further it moves along the path of purification and perfection.

CHAPTER SIX

The Islamic Paradigm

An Islamic paradigm is necessary for Islamic universities and for the production of Islamic knowledge. It should be a holistic, comprehensive, and integrated paradigm that can encompass the wholeness of Islamic thought. From an educational perspective, the Islamic worldview can be translated into the following components that can capture the uniqueness and the wholeness of the Islamic school of thought and produce Islamic knowledge.

The Islamic paradigm includes (1) Islamic spiritual psychology; (2) epistemology; (3) ontology; (4) eschatology; (5) sociology; and (6) methodology. The common theme in all the components of the paradigm is the principle of *tawḥīd*. The Islamic paradigm can be defined as a holistic, integrated paradigm. On the one hand, it is divine, spiritual, religious, eternal, constant, absolute, and ideal. On the other, it is human, material, rational, temporary, mutable, and relative. These two opposites are intimately interwoven by the dialectics of *tawḥīd*.

The principles underlying the Islamic paradigm are discussed in detail in the following sections.

ISLAMIC SPIRITUAL PSYCHOLOGY: UNITY OF THE SELF

A sound holistic system is possible only when it is built on the firm psychological nature of the human being. According to the Islamic school of thought, people are God's vicegerents on earth and have the potential of being higher than the angels.

Islam sees humankind as the vicegerency of God on earth and the projection, as it were, of the vertical dimension and the horizontal plane. Gifted with intelligence in the true sense of the term, humans alone of all creatures are capable of knowing the reality, of which they themselves are a manifestation, and, in the light of this knowledge, of rising above their own earthly and contingent selfhood.

Gifted with the power of speech, he alone stands before God as His
valid interlocutor. Through Revelation as also through inspiration
God speaks to His creation, through prayer as also through an awareness which is a silent form of communication, man speaks to God and
does so on behalf of the inarticulate creation that surrounds him. He
is, potentially if not actually, higher that the angels are, for his nature
reflects totality and can be satisfied with nothing less than the total.[1]

Because of the position granted to the human being in Islam, any
Islamic education system should first acknowledge and develop integrated human beings. The education system should address the Muslim learner as a whole person who possesses a body, mind, and soul,
and prepare the various faculties of that person to realize the wholeness of life and hence the unity of the Divine Principle.

ISLAMIC EPISTEMOLOGY: UNITY OF KNOWLEDGE

The second principle in the Islamic paradigm deals with the unity of
knowledge. Unity and awareness of the self lead to the realization of
the unity of God's knowledge. A holistic education should lead its followers through observation and reflection on nature to understand
the unity that connects God's creation. A holistic education integrates
and unites the spiritual and the physical. Spirituality never opposes the
use of matter.

Rather, it always makes use of the formal, which it interiorizes. Also,
the spiritual cannot be simply equated with the esoteric as opposed to
the exoteric. Although the spiritual is more closely related to the esoteric dimension *al-bāṭin* of Islam than to any other aspect of the
religion, it is also very much concerned with the exoteric acts and the
Divine Law as well as theology, philosophy, the arts and sciences created by Islam and its civilization. But its concern with the exoteric is
always a journey from the outward to the abode of inwards.[2]

Thus a holistic curriculum should be established on a Qur'anic
foundation that integrates physical, scientific, and religious/spiritual
knowledge. The theories of knowledge of Ibn Sīnā and al-Ghazālī are
built on a Qur'anic foundation. An analysis of the classification of
knowledge by Ibn Sīnā will show the reflection of Qur'anic teaching
and the emphasis on the life-transaction and this world (*al-dīn wa*

al-dunya). The concept of the perennial and the temporal, this-world-ly and the other-worldly, is included in Ibn Sīnā's classification of knowledge, which reflects his theory of knowledge. Both scholars rec-ognize knowledge as temporal and perennial, but perennial know-ledge is the goal for which Muslims should strive. Table 6.1 shows the classification of knowledge according to Ibn Sīnā.

Ibn Sīnā defined the aim of *theoretical philosophy* – the perfecting of the soul through knowledge – as "the occurrence of positive belief of things," whereas the aims of *practical philosophy* were defined not only as the perfecting of the soul through knowledge, but also as act-ing in accordance with the requirements of that knowledge. The aim of theoretical philosophy, therefore, is *truth*, whereas the aim of prac-tical philosophy is *goodness*.

Ibn Sīnā divided theoretical philosophy into three kinds of sciences according to the degree of their connection with matter and motion or their independence of them:

1. natural sciences, which he called the lowest sciences;
2. mathematical sciences, which he called the middle sciences;
3. theological or metaphysical sciences, which he called
    the highest sciences;
    that is, according to their abstraction and independence from matter.

Practical philosophy was also divided into three branches of knowl-edge:

1. ethics or morality (*akhlāq*), which is concerned with the management of human behavior as an individual or the purity of oneself;
2. household management (*ʿilm tadbīr al-manzil*) or the pragmatism of a man as a member of a family, which is concerned with the relationship of a man to his wife, his children, and his domestic staff, as well as the manage-ment of a livelihood and family income;
3. public management (*ʿilm tadbīr al-madīnah*) or the prag-matism of a man as a member of a community, which is

concerned with the politics of a city, a state, as well as a community of states.

What characterized classic Muslim philosophers was their knowledge of a wide range of disciplines and, at the same time, their ability to unify the diversity and realize the unity of God's knowledge. It is spirituality and the dialectical concept of *tawḥīd* that creates wholeness and unity in self and in knowledge.

The Classification of Knowledge According to Ibn Sīnā[3]
[Table 6.1]

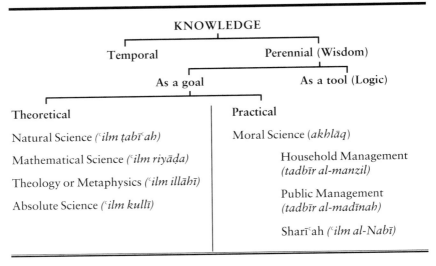

ISLAMIC ONTOLOGY AND METAPHYSICS:
UNITY OF COSMOS AND NATURAL ORDER

The third principle in the Islamic paradigm is the realization of the unity of nature, the physical universe, and the metaphysical realms. Reflection on the cosmos and the natural order illuminates the spiritual facets of relationships between people and the world around them. The Qur'an invites people to reflect on the signs in nature as well as on those within themselves to realize the underlying unity between these interrelated orders of reality. The emphasis, in terms of spiritual development, is strongly placed on the illumination of the inward signs.

Islamic spirituality is therefore based not only upon the reading of the written Qur'an *al-Qur'ān al-tadwīnī* but also upon deciphering the text of the cosmic Qur'an *al-Qur'ān al-takwīnī*, which is its complement. Nature in Islamic spirituality is, consequently, not the adversary but the friend of the traveler upon the spiritual path and an aid to the person of spiritual vision in the journey through his forms to the world of the Spirit, which is the origin of both man and Cosmos.4

The concept of nature finds its appropriate place in the overall context of Islamic cosmology, which acts as a bridge connecting pure metaphysics with the branches of science that deal with the physical world. The study of nature, therefore, can reveal an aspect of Divine Wisdom, provided that such a study does not divorce the world from its Divine Principle. Thus, an Islamic holistic curriculum built on the concept of nature is able to plant in the learner's mind and soul the seeds of the oneness and unity of the Divine Principle. Relating the secrets of the soul to the unity of God's Knowledge and the signs in the cosmic order connects students to the concept of *tawḥīd* and leads them to realizing Divine Wisdom and the significance of life and death. Realization of the relationship between the microcosm and macrocosm should be developed as a major principle in the Islamic paradigm.

> We shall show them our portents [*āyāt*] upon the horizon and within themselves, until it becomes manifest unto them that it is the Truth. (The Qur'an, 41:53)

ISLAMIC ESCHATOLOGY: UNITY OF LIFE

The fourth principle in the Islamic paradigm is realization of the final destination. The theme of the hereafter can be discussed under Islamic epistemology in the religious classification, but it is discussed here because of its importance. The hereafter is one of the most fundamental themes in the Qur'an. The concept of the hereafter is important in Islamic holistic education because it enhances the spirituality of learners by directing their attention to the other world. In addition, by presenting the themes of the hereafter and the here-and-now at the same time, students are able to see the importance of both this world and the other world, helping them to develop their dialectical thinking and to keep the balance between the two opposing ideas. The here-after is always discussed in the Qur'an in relation to this world:

> Linguistically it is not possible in the Qur'an to talk about one [world] without reference to the other [world] since every term used for each is comparative with the other. Thus: *al-ūlā* and *al-ākhira* (the first and the last); *al-dunya* and *al-akhīra* (the Nearer and the Further/Last). Neither has a name specific to itself that does not refer to the other. Consequently the frequency of occurrence in the Qur'an is the same, in the case of *dunya* and *akhira*: 115 times.5

The Muslims are reminded continually of the hereafter so that they may not lose sight of the essence of their existence in this world. To deny the next life is to ascribe futility to Divine Wisdom in creation: "Did you think that We created you in vain and that you would not be returned to us?" (The Qur'an, 23:115).

The theme of the hereafter provides Muslims with the concept of the final destination of the journey of life. It presents the totality and the vision of the journey of perfection and search for unity. The theme of the hereafter inculcates spirituality in Muslims' actions throughout their lives if they follow the words of God. More importantly, the differences between this world and the other world develop students' dialectical thinking along the lines of *tawḥīd*, moving souls and minds toward a state of equilibrium and contentment. "In the Islamic view, the human perfection realized when the soul attains to the stage of peace with God means that the will of the individual is totally integrated into the Divine will."6

ISLAMIC SOCIOLOGY: UNITY OF THE COMMUNITY

The fifth principle in the Islamic paradigm is related to the community and society in general. The development of human beings in Islam is emphasized not only because it leads to the perfection of individuals, but also because it is intimately related to the perfection of society so as to fulfill collectively the Divine Will. Islam realizes the importance of collective action for the fulfillment of any task. It is not only a religion that teaches about spirituality and purification of the individual soul, it is also a complete social system whose laws are stated in the

Sacred Text. Wholeness, once more, proves itself in the Qur'anic school. The intimate relationship between the individual and society is another level of the wholeness of Islam: such a holistic approach takes account of the mutual effects that society and the individual have on each other.

ISLAMIC METHODOLOGY OF *TAWḤĪD*: THE ULTIMATE UNITY

The sixth principle in the paradigm is fostering the concept of *tawḥīd*. According to Islamic thought an eternal Divine principle of unity pervades and rules all things. It is expressed in the metaphysical world of the hereafter and the Day of Judgment, in the external world of cosmos and nature, and in the inner world of mind and spirit. Underlying this universal order of things is a living unity, which is all-pervading and everlasting. Everything has a purpose, which is realization of the essence of the Divine nature developing within it, to prepare the soul for receiving the Divine Truth. To be able to realize and reveal the essence of one's being and of existence in general, Islam points its followers to the path for realizing the essence of life. *Tawḥīd* is the path that reveals the unity of God. *Tawḥīd* is the essence and spirit of Islam. It is through the dialectic of *tawḥīd* that Muslims accept contradiction in their beings, nature and universe around them. It is the concept of *tawḥīd* that keeps the balance among diverse multiplicities and contradictions. Finally, *tawḥīd* gives Islam its spirituality by reminding its followers of the ultimate goal of this life.

In his introduction to *Islamic Spirituality*, Nasr states:

> The spirit manifests itself in every religion where the echoes of the Divine world are still available, but the manner in which the manifestations of the spirit take place differs from one religion to another. In Islam the spirit breathes through all that reveals the One and leads to the One, for Islam's ultimate purpose is to reveal the Unity of the Divine Principle and to integrate the world of multiplicity in the light of that Unity. Spirituality in Islam is inseparable from the awareness of the One, of Allah, and a life lived according to His Will.[7]

Therefore, rooting the holistic curriculum in the concept of *tawḥīd* and using it as a method of enquiry will develop students' dialectical thinking. From an educational point of view, this mode of inquiry enhances students' critical thinking.

Therefore, acquiring knowledge, thinking, reflection, and contemplation are only one dimension of the development of human beings. The knowledge acquired should be translated into something more concrete that can be utilized to serve humanity. Thus action is the other dimension of the Islamic school of thought; contemplation and action are two interrelated principles in Islam. Both knowledge and action should lead to the attainment of the ultimate goal, which is the perfection of human beings, which leads to the realization of the Divine Principle of Unity. The path that leads from the acquiring of knowledge to the execution of action is ethics and morality. Al-Ghazālī's theory of ethics describes in detail the moral issues of knowledge and action.[8]

In brief, the Islamic paradigm is all-encompassing, developmental, purposeful, and integrated. It is based on the Qur'anic school of thought and derives its principles from the Sacred Text. All the principles of the Islamic paradigm lead to the realization of the Unity of the Divine Principle. Spiritual psychology integrates body, mind, and soul as one unified whole. Because Islamic epistemology is holistic, it addresses the material and the scientific as well as the religious and spiritual aspects of knowledge. In addition, Islamic ontology and metaphysics address the wholeness of the cosmos and the natural order. The Islamic paradigm deals with nature and universal laws scientifically and spiritually. Moreover, Islamic eschatology deals with both the hereafter and the here-and-now. This draws students to think of both worlds, but to remember that this world is the means to be cultivated to an end, which is the hereafter. Islamic sociology deals with social and community issues: it is considered to be the duty of each individual to participate in, develop, and improve societal life. More importantly, individuals are responsible for maintaining the unity of society.

Finally, Islamic methodology of *tawḥīd* helps Muslim students to understand the controversial issues involved in life and in education. It also helps their dialectical and critical thinking which are considered the highest stage of adult development. Therefore, an Islamic holistic education system should further these goals.

CHAPTER SEVEN

Islamic Epistemology: Gateway to Knowledge

Islamic epistemology is presented in this chapter from an educational point of view, rather than a philosophical or theoretical perspective. The intention is to make Islamic epistemology accessible to Muslim students and scholars of all university faculties. The focus is on the structure of Islamic epistemology, how students can relate to it, and how they can understand from an Islamic perspective the knowledge to which they are exposed in the West. I am aiming, also, to highlight the wholeness of Islamic epistemology and the unity of knowledge and self in Islam. Finally, I am hoping that Muslim students and scholars at Western universities will develop their own framework for understanding, analyzing, and interpreting their studies from an Islamic perspective. If students and scholars wish to know more about the philosophical bases of Islamic epistemology, they can refer to original or translated sources of Islamic philosophy and Islamic epistemology.

Bringing down epistemology from its ivory tower to the classroom is not an easy task. However, I have tried not to simplify the concept, but to discover and reveal practical dimensions of Islamic epistemology. As a teacher, I always try to find the practical side of any theory and apply it to real life. My main concern about Muslim students in Western universities is that they are cut off completely from their Islamic knowledge at university level.

However, I must admit that Muslim scholars and graduate students are in a unique position for producing and developing Islamic science and Islamic knowledge in Western universities. They have the best research facilities and unlimited access to information. North American and European universities are equipped with the latest information and communication technology that serve as the backbone of any research. Libraries have millions of books in many languages and on all subjects. Arabic books to which we should never

have access in the Middle East are available in Western universities. As
Muslim educators and scholars, we have an obligation toward our
Muslim students in the West. Our obligation, in my opinion, is to
make Islamic knowledge accessible to our students in all fields, not
only to those who major in Islamic studies. Wholeness of knowledge
and the self should be emphasized, and holiness too, focusing on the
importance of keeping the integrity of our intellectual and spiritual
identity. What made Islamic science unique fourteen centuries ago
was this wholeness and its basis in the Islamic teachings of the Divine
Book. In this context, al-Ghazālī's theory of knowledge is presented
in this chapter as a model for Islamic epistemology.

AL-GHAZĀLĪ'S THEORY OF KNOWLEDGE

Al-Ghazālī's theory of knowledge derives from the philosophy of Ibn
Sīnā and al-Fārābī. However, the source of any Islamic epistemology is
the Divine Book. *Tawḥīd*, unity of oneness, is the essence of Islamic
epistemology for it is the essence of Islam itself. By now we know that
Islamic epistemology is both religious and other-worldly, and materially oriented and this-worldly. It is divided into theoretical and
practical knowledge, but it leads in one direction and fulfills the wholeness of human life, cosmos, and the relationship between them. This
simple, yet complex, concept is summarized in the Qur'an as *al-dunya
wa al-ākhira* (this world and the other world). The Islamic theory of
knowledge includes religious and spiritual issues dealing with God, the
soul, the unseen world, the angels, ʿilm al-mukāshafah, and other
metaphysical subjects, as well as material or worldly issues (ʿilm al-
muʿāmalah). Western secular epistemology cannot and would not
tolerate such wholeness. Wholeness, complexity, and contradictions
represent chaos and uncertainty from a Western positivist perspective.
These issues were discussed in detail in Chapter 3, under its review of
paradigms.

   Al-Ghazālī, as a classic theologian, philosopher, and teacher at the
Nizāmiyyah in Baghdad in the tenth century AC, had the qualities necessary to develop a balanced theory of knowledge. In addition, after
Ibn Miskawayh, al-Ghazālī was the first Muslim to introduce and
develop a theory of virtue and ethics, and he used his theory of ethics

as a path between knowledge and action. Tibawi believes that al-Ghazālī's theory of knowledge was the most comprehensive and systematic in classical Arabic literature[1].

In the *Book of Knowledge*, al-Ghazālī explains that the knowledge that leads us, as human beings, safely to the hereafter is the only praiseworthy knowledge. He goes on to divide knowledge into the religious (*ʿulūm sharʿiyyah*) and the rational (*ʿulūm ʿaqliyyah*). The latter refers to knowledge attained solely by the human intellect, and the former, the knowledge received from the prophets. He states in his *Iḥyāʾ ʿUlūm al-Dīn* (Revival of Religious Sciences) that although both religious and rational knowledge is important for achieving purification of the mind and the soul, the ultimate aim of knowledge, however, is purification of the soul. An important aspect of al-Ghazālī's theory of knowledge is his theory of virtue, which he classified under religious sciences; it was discussed in Chapter 2.

Islamic epistemology embodies wholeness and holiness for it embraces both the religious and material as one whole. It is holy because of the religious component, especially the theory of virtue, containing all of the virtues that can transform any knowledge to holiness. In his quest for truth, al-Ghazālī emphasized that the criterion for any knowledge is its usefulness in leading human beings to those moral states that facilitate the attainment of ultimate happiness. So ethics provides the link between knowledge and action, between the philosophical and the practical. Knowledge can be dangerous if it is not associated with ethics. For example, genetic engineering is a dangerous piece of knowledge that, if stripped of ethics and morality, could lead to disastrous results.

THE HOLISTIC VIEW OF KNOWLEDGE

Islamic epistemology is deeply rooted in religion and spirituality. Therefore, any attempt to introduce a theory of knowledge into Islamic societies which does not take into account religion and spirituality side by side with the scientific, material, and rational will be one-dimensional and will not fulfill the needs of Muslim students. Islam is not only a religion; it is a complete way of life. A human being, from an Islamic point of view, possesses a body, mind, and soul.

Islamic epistemology, therefore, takes into account this fact and builds its theories accordingly. A purely materialistic and rationalistic epistemology which takes only mind and matter into account and which draws its experiences from the senses is not suitable for Muslims simply because it does not address an important part of their being – and does not teach them how to deal with it. An idealistic epistemology, which considers only a person's soul and inner being, will not suit Muslims either because it will neglect the mind, intellect, body, and the material dimension of life. Thus, neither a pure material nor a pure idealistic epistemology is appropriate for the Muslim world.

An Islamic epistemology is required to fulfill the needs of both the religious and material dimensions of life. Such an epistemology should be rooted in religion, philosophy, science, and technology. It has to be comprehensive and holistic, dealing with all aspects of both the knower and the known. Such an epistemology takes into consideration the fact that there is a *real world*, in which we live, and an ideal world, for which we strive. Mutahhari states that the realities perceived by the senses are phenomena from which the following five properties are inseparable: limitation, change, dependency, need, and relativity.[2] All of these properties belong to the real, relative world in which we live and the universe and people that surround us. For this reason, Islamic epistemology takes into account the limitations, mutability, and relativity of the real world as only one dimension of the theory of knowledge.

Besides the real world in which we live, there is an ideal or 'unseen world' which, according to Islam, is the world for which we strive. The belief in the unseen is essential to Islamic faith. God, his angels, the Day of Judgment, and the hereafter are all 'unseen.' It is the duty of Muslims to believe in them, not blindly, but through search, and reflection on God's creation, guided by the Sacred Text. It is a commonplace methodology, starting from the concrete to reach the abstract, from the known to discover the unknown. The Qur'an makes repeated acknowledgment of the unseen: "Those who believe in the unseen..." (2:2); "With Him are the keys to the unseen – none knows them but He" (6:59). The unseen world challenges Muslims to move from the concrete to the abstract. This movement is defined by some psychologists as the highest stage of adult development. The goal of human beings, according to Islam, is to try to reach that ideal through knowledge of the self, the universe, and God, and through good deeds, that is, to put their knowledge into action which must be bound by morality.

Ibn Sīnā (Avicenna), the tenth-century Muslim philosopher, in his theory of knowledge "distinguishes between a 'potential intellect' in human beings and an 'active intellect' outside human being, through the influence and guidance of which the former develops and matures."[3] So the potential intellect in human beings tries to understand, analyze, and rationalize, while God will shed some light on human beings' intellect to help them to understand and find answers to their questions.

Ibn Sīnā thus declares that the task for our minds is to consider and reflect upon the particulars of sense experience. This activity prepares the mind for the reception of the Universal essence from the active intellect by an act of direct intuition. The perception of the universal form, then, is a unique movement of the intellective soul, not reducible to our perceiving the particulars either singly or totally and finding the common essence among them; if this were so, it would be only a spurious kind of universal.

> The origin of knowledge is mysterious and involves intuition at every stage. Of all intellectual knowledge, more or less, it is not so much true to say "I know it" as to admit, "It occurs to me." All seeking for knowledge, according to Ibn Sīnā, has this prayer-like quality: the effort is necessary on the part of man; the response is the act of God as the active intellect. We are, indeed, often not aware as to what it is we want to know, let alone go ahead and 'know' it.[4]

It was not a miracle when Islamic civilization flourished and produced great scholars at certain periods. The main reason for such a flow of knowledge in all disciplines was the consistency in the Islamic worldview, philosophy, and epistemology, which was reflected in Islamic education that accommodated both religious and material needs. The miracle, however, is in the consistency, harmony, and connectedness of the Qur'an, which is, according to Muslims, the only and absolute source of knowledge and truth and because the Qur'an is the Word of God. A review of the Islamic worldview and epistemology shows clearly the inconsistency, lack of harmony, and disconnectedness in current Islamic societies and in Western, secular higher education systems that are transplanted from the West.

Realizing the importance of all sciences – what he identified as 'rational sciences' and 'religious sciences' – al-Ghazālī established a firm foundation, from his epistemology, on which to build Islamic education. Knowledge of sciences dealing with things that God has made is regarded by al-Ghazālī as a necessary prelude to the knowledge of God Himself. Al-Ghazālī in his book, *Mīzān al-ʿAmal*, states:

> If the soul has not been exercised in the sciences dealing with fact and demonstration, it will acquire mental phantasms, which will be mistaken by it to be truth descending upon it…Many Sufis remain stuck for years in such figments of imagination, but they certainly would have been saved from these, had they first followed the path of scientific study and acquired by laborious learning as much at the demonstrative sciences as human power could encompass.5

Umaruddin explains that knowledge, according to al-Ghazālī, has two aspects: formal and existential.6 The formal is innate and is the knowledge of the form in which the various objects of experience and intuition are understood. It is the knowledge of self-evident principles. It is not based on experience; it is a priori. Existential knowledge is acquired and is the knowledge of objects and events attained from experience and intuition. Existential knowledge is of two kinds: phenomenal and spiritual. The former is the knowledge of the material world, whereas the latter is knowledge of spiritual realities, such as God, the soul, and angels. According to al-Ghazālī, knowledge of spiritual realities is the highest form of knowledge and depends on intuition. Intellect and knowledge develop with age from practical and intuitive experiences.

An awareness of such a classification of knowledge and its components of both the physical and the metaphysical helps students and educators to acquire knowledge that enables them to develop holistically – both intellectually and spiritually.

KNOWLEDGE AND ISLAM

Knowledge in Islam is considered to be sacred because it has always been associated with God's words. Besides, learning and teaching in Islam started in the mosques. The most prominent 'houses of knowledge' or 'houses of wisdom' and academies were established in the mosques or attached to them. Education always started with learning the Qur'an. So, from the early days, Islam associated knowledge with the Sacred Text. That meant that the Qur'an was not kept on the shelf, to be taken down and read only at prayer times or on special occasions. On the contrary, this sanctification meant that one was to take the Qur'an seriously, to read, study, analyze, reflect on, and discover its hidden treasures.

The power and mystery of the Qur'an lies in its universality and its comprehensiveness. It is not restricted to time or place. People from all walks of life can relate to it and understand it. The language, the concepts, and the meanings of the Qur'an are both simple and complex. They are multilevel and multidimensional. On the one hand, ordinary people can understand it and consider it their constitution for running their personal, spiritual, social, economic, and political lives, and in understanding their relationships with God, people, and the universe around them. On the other hand, the Qur'an has proved to be the most difficult and complex Book, which, throughout the ages, has puzzled the powerful minds of Muslim philosophers, scientists, linguists, and theologians. It is in the Qur'an that scientists, philosophers, and theologians have found their theories and produced their encyclopedic works on metaphysics, philosophy, and the unseen world, medicine, astronomy, mathematics, anatomy, and the psyche, the nature of plants, animals, and minerals, just to mention some of the works of Muslim scholars.

The entire Islamic civilization was built on the Qur'an. It may be hard to believe that such a great and dazzling civilization was built on only one Book, but it is a fact. Islam means 'submission to truth.'[7] According to Islamic teachings, the word of God is the Ultimate Truth. Islamic civilization means the civilization that submitted itself to the truth, to the word of God. In the divine school of God, the

Qur'an was the only Book and the Prophet was the first teacher. In this Qur'anic school, Islamic intellect reached its full flowering: illustrious, towering figures flourished in all the sciences and created and accumulated a huge body of knowledge. Muslim scholars always acknowledged the influence of Greek, Indian, and Persian civilizations on their work. But this love of knowledge, the honesty in reporting the references, and loyalty to the sources of their knowledge are Qur'anic characteristics. It is the Sacred Text that encourages people to seek knowledge and truth, and there are prophetic traditions that state: "seek knowledge from the cradle to the tomb" and "seek knowledge, even if it is in China."

> Verily, in the creation of the heavens and the earth, and in the succession of night and day; and the ships that run upon the sea with what is useful to mankind; and the water that God sends down from heaven wherewith He revives the earth after its being dead; and His spreading over it all kinds of creatures; and the changing directions of the winds; and clouds compelled between heaven and the earth; verily, these are signs for people who comprehend. (The Qur'an, 2:164)

Almost all of the great Muslim philosophers and scientists were strong believers in God. One characteristic which distinguished Muslim scholars was their multifaceted scholarship. They wanted to discover and experience the truth from different angles and from different dimensions. The main reason behind their perseverance was that God asked them to be so and challenged them to discover the consistency of God's words.

> Who created the seven heavens, tallied, You do not see in the creation of the Most Benignant any discrepancy, return your gaze: do you see any crevice? (The Qur'an, 67:3)

Therefore, many Muslim philosophers were well versed in several other disciplines. Sharif states that besides writing on philosophy, al-Kindī also wrote, to name only the main subjects, upon astrology, chemistry, optics, and music; al-Fārābī, on music, psychology, politics, economics, and mathematics; Ibn Sīnā, on medicine, chemistry, geometry, astronomy, theology, poetry, and music; Zakariyā al-Rāzī, on medicine and alchemy; al-Ghazālī on theology, law, physics, ethics, psychology, and music; Ikhwān al-Ṣafā on mathematics, astronomy, geography, music, and ethics.[8] This is to mention only a few Muslim philosophers and scholars.

WHOLENESS AND HOLINESS IN ISLAMIC EDUCATION

If we agree that the two opposing yet complementary concepts of *al-dunya wa al-ākhira* (this world and the other world), religious and material, relative and absolute, embody the Qur'anic concepts of wholeness and holiness, then education from an Islamic point of view should be based on them, for they lead to the right path (*al ṣirāt al-mustaqīm*). To seek knowledge is obligatory for all Muslim men and women, to know God, our inner selves, and the cosmos. Thus Islamic education is tridimensional. It comprises God, the human being, and the cosmos, God being the Ultimate Truth; the human being the seeker of that Truth; and the cosmos, the multidimensional means and environment that can be utilized by human beings to reveal God's love and the Universal Soul that shines throughout the universe if we are open to listening and understanding. Education in general has lost its connection with spirituality and the absolute truth.

> The unifying vision with which related knowledge to love and faith, religion to science, and theology to all the departments of intellectual concerns is finally completely lost, leaving a world of compartmentalization where there is no wholeness because holiness has ceased to be of central concern, or is at best reduced to sentimentality.[9]

In this section I shall shed some light on the relationship between the three dimensions of Islamic education: the human being, the cosmos, and God. However, the focus is on human beings and the cosmos: human beings as the seekers of knowledge and the cosmos as the means of discovering that knowledge. The discussion starts with human beings as the center of this world and God's vicegerents on earth.

The focus will be on how we as human beings relate to our inner selves and how we develop that relationship. The questions that I am trying to answer are these: What is an inner relationship? Why do I need to connect and relate to myself? How do I connect and relate to myself? How does that fit into Islamic epistemology? I shall explain why I am using human beings as the starting point and not God nor the cosmos.

Secondly, I shall explain our relationship to the cosmos and why I choose to deal with it at this point as a second element in the Islamic paradigm. Questions regarding the cosmos – *what*, *why*, and *how* – are discussed and related to nature and the cosmos. What is the importance of all this to our understanding of ourselves, the other, nature, and God? Can reflection on nature as physical and material phenomena relate us to God (the invisible and nonphysical), to reach and understand the metaphysical, God, angels, and the other world? Can it be the medium that transforms the physical into the metaphysical, the concrete into the abstract?

Finally, I shall discuss the importance of knowing God and building a relationship with Him. What does it mean to know God and to build a relationship with Him? *Why* do we have to know God and to understand Him? *What* are the means by which we can know God? Can we know God through our minds only? Or our intuition only? *How* can we develop these concepts in our daily lives and our education?

STARTING WITH OURSELVES

Starting with ourselves is extremely important on the long journey to self-realization and the fulfillment of the goal of our being in this world. It is common sense that one cannot relate to others or understand them if one cannot relate to oneself. Unfortunately the present education system all over the world is separating individuals from their real selves. Students and teachers feel alienated in their own homes and their own schools because neither the subject matter nor teaching methods are such that one would feel any connection with or passion for the subjects. Memorizing theories and formulae or knowing them just does not promote real learning.

Learning becomes real and meaningful when it is related to real things in people's lives, when it enables the learners to ask real questions about life. Learners become passionate about their learning when issues discussed in the classroom set them on journeys to discover their inner and intimate selves. Although our personal experiences connect us to spiritual, social, and political issues, they have to start from the core of our being. The more intense the personal experience, the more embedded it becomes in constructing meanings. Much of what we learn entails making new interpretations that enable us to tolerate further differences, and reinforce or deconstruct our long-established frames of reference or create new meaning schemes. Perhaps even more central to us as learners than elaborating established meaning schemes is the process of reflecting on prior learning to determine whether what we have learned is justified under present circumstances.

So reflection on personal experiences helps us, as learners, to understand past experiences and reconstruct them in the light of new knowledge or experiences. Reflection helps us to recall past experiences, to analyze them, and to go beyond the experience to see the meaning, and sometimes to transfer the whole experience to a higher level of understanding. Reflection on our experiences assists us in understanding how and why we perceived, felt, or acted as we did, and in assessing the value of our experiences. So, in brief, reflection refines the quality of our experiences. By understanding and finding meaning in our past experiences we honor them and improve the quality of future experiences. We become more aware and more sensitive and more connected to our inner souls. When we are reflecting we are connecting directly to our minds, our bodies, and our souls.

By reflection and contemplation we become whole and sometimes we become holy, in the sense that we connect to the Universal Soul. In the Divine Revelation, the Qur'an, God urges us to reflect on ourselves and nature to make meaning and to understand. So in reflection we start to understand our real selves, our silent serene souls that have been neglected.

Reflection, in some cases, can elevate us to the state of prayer. We feel that our souls are cleansing themselves from impurities imposed on them by our irresponsible actions and lifestyles. Even when our souls cry out for help, we either neglect them or we cannot hear their voices. When we look into our souls we see that they are buried under jealousy, hatred, aggression, and worldly desires and demands. Such turmoil disconnects us severely from our souls; they become alien to us and we to them.

An inner relationship, therefore, is an intimate, spiritual relationship between the person and her or his soul. It is a state of wholeness and holiness. It is a preparatory stage to becoming a whole person so as to be able to perceive reality holistically, and to be able to realize and understand the Absolute Truth. Purifying the soul and disciplining it is to prepare it for connection to its original source: to God.

The more we are sincere in becoming a whole person, the greater our chances of perceiving and understanding reality as it is. This will answer my second question: *Why do we need to connect to our selves?* If, as human beings, we are disconnected and fragmented, and our minds, bodies, and souls are not in harmony, we shall not be able to understand the real meaning of life, we shall not be able to know why we are in this world, the purpose of our being, and where we are heading. We shall be trapped in daily triviality, the demands of the body, and the complexity of the mind. Our energy is sapped in looking after the physical and mental daily demands, while ignoring the demands of the soul. So the need to initiate a relationship with our inner selves is a need to put ourselves together after being disconnected from ourselves by the education system, the media, and the destructive Western style of living and thinking.

The education system distorts the mind with the positivistic paradigm and the 'scientific' statistical research methods used to produce distorted knowledge. The results of such fragmented, reductionist knowledge are obvious. The environment is suffering: the forests are suffering, and oceans, seas, lakes, rivers, and all the creatures in the waters are suffering. The Western 'destructive civilization,' as Sardar calls it, has destroyed the ozone layer by its irresponsible, aggressive, inhuman approaches to science and discovery.[10] Western scientific destruction has reached the deepest part of the ocean, the poles of the sphere, and all that is in between. Nothing has been spared from scientific and technological destruction; even the human soul, body, and mind have all been experimented upon and tampered with under the guise of scientific and technological advancement.

So we, as humans, need to connect to our inner selves to be able to have insight and wisdom, to develop a caring attitude to all that surrounds us. Nature is not our enemy to be conquered, raped, tortured, and assaulted, just to satisfy fully our animalistic desires no matter what damage we are causing. Connecting to our inner souls allows us to experience and be aware of the beauty lying silently and profoundly inside us. We touch our spirituality and realize how precious, valuable, and indispensable we are to ourselves. We start learning to care for ourselves and love ourselves. In rare moments of intense spirituality, when God's Soul touches our soul and only we know it is real, nothing can be the same again. It is a state of realization and awakening; it is deep, real, and beautiful. When we care for our souls, we start caring for others, for nature, and for everything surrounding us; we start caring with love and the 'ethical love' becomes 'natural love.'

The third question that I am trying to answer is: *How* do we relate and connect to our inner selves? From an early age, children are taught to pray, fast, read the Qur'an, give charity, and help others. They learn to respect parents, the elderly, and their teachers. In any Muslim society that observes religion, Islam is the center of all activities. This has been explained in detail in Chapter 1, 'Reflection on Personal Experiences.'

So from the early years, a Muslim child starts asking questions about God, the angels, and facts about life and death. These questions allow the child to go deep into herself or himself and reflect on the answers received from parents. Thus religion and spirituality become part of the child's life. By observing and practicing daily rituals, children gradually evolve inwardly and establish a relationship with God and the unseen world. Certainty is *not* among the teachings that one receives in a Muslim home. Uncertainty, as a matter of fact, is what is taught and practiced. Of course many Islamic concepts have been misunderstood and abused, such as *inshā'Allāh*. The phrase means 'God willing' and is an expression used at the end of a statement to mean: "This is my plan, but I am not certain what is going to happen; only God knows."

COSMOS, THE EN RULE (–) IN THE 'I–THOU' RELATIONSHIP

The second dimension of Islamic education is the cosmos. In this study the cosmos is considered the metaphysical principle that connects human beings to themselves, to God, and the 'other.' The 'other' can be other people, nature, or other objects. In the present discussion, I draw mainly on Nasr's writings on cosmology.[11]

> Traditional cosmology does not only concern the macrocosm but also the microcosm. It contains a complete knowledge of the soul as it does of the qualitative aspect of the Universe...The traditional cosmologies are related to man's inner perfection and to his ultimate end...They provide the background for that process of spiritual maturing which enables man to become God's vicegerent in actuality rather than only potentially and thus to fulfill his role vis a vis nature as its protector.[12]

Nature can be considered the physical image of the cosmos, which allows us as humans to discover natural and physical laws and to understand the cosmos and its metaphysical principles. By connecting to our souls through reflection, contemplation, and prayer, we are one step closer to fulfilling our role in this life, that is, to become the vicegerents of God on this earth. In the previous section I explained the importance of connecting and relating to ourselves as human beings, to become one whole as God first created us. The same applies to our realization of the cosmos as one whole, integrated body of knowledge. Therefore, wholeness is an essential principle for the understanding of the One and the many.

As has been explained earlier, cosmology is placed in this chapter between humans and God as the environment that allows us to relate to God through the physical and the metaphysical to reach higher levels of understanding. Cosmological principles have many applications in Islamic sciences. They are related, on the one hand, to the physical world and the natural environment. On the other hand, they are bound closely to the metaphysical world and knowledge of a higher order. They are like invisible threads that hold all of the elements to form the whole. For this reason the cosmos is considered the en rule '–' in the 'I–Thou' relationship as expressed by Buber. Human beings come to know their inner selves and God by reflecting on nature and the universe.

"We shall show them our portents on the horizon and within themselves until it will be manifested unto them that it is the Truth" (The Qur'an, 41:53). Nasr states:

In all forms of cosmology, however, the aim has remained the same, namely to transfer the cosmos and its parts into an 'icon' which can be revealed within the matrix in which the ONE can be revealed within the matrix of multiplicity itself. Beginning with the Universe which has been transformed by the Qur'anic revelation, the universe in which the Archangel Gabriel descended and the Prophet made his nocturnal ascent (*al-miʿrāj*) to the Divine Proximity...Islamic cosmology, therefore, displays many facts and forms but all leading to a single inner content. The meaning of all the cosmological schemes in Islam has remained the same, namely the relating of multiplicity to unity...

The 'night of power' (*laylat al-qadr*), during which the Qur'an was revealed, and the 'night of ascent' (*laylat al-miʿrāj*) complement each other and signify from the cosmological point of view the Islamicization of the cosmos in the descending and ascending orders, or from the cosmogonic and initiatic point of view.[13]

In the Holy Book of Islam, God teaches us directly and indirectly how to reflect on natural phenomena and universal phenomena so as to learn lessons and to see God's signs everywhere. The cosmos and its principles, which are rooted in metaphysics and branched in all other sciences, were given by God to humanity to be used for higher knowledge and higher purposes. All natural phenomena are provided by God to be used, not abused. Reflection and meditation connect us to our inner selves, to see and realize the microcosm inside us, and eventually to connect to God and realize His ultimate Love. The 'night of ascent' (*laylat al-miʿrāj*) was a physical and concrete sign of God Almighty to show human beings where they could ascend if they realized their position and potential.

Therefore, the exchange between earth and heaven – of the descent of the Archangel Gabriel to the earth and the ascent of the Prophet through the seven heavens to the Divine Throne – reflects in practice what human beings can attain if they are open to receiving God's Love and His Knowledge, which in fact reside inside them. These two powerful events illustrate the relationship between human beings, the cosmos, and God. They also illustrate the position of the human being as both God's vicegerent (*khalīfat Allāh*) and God's servant (*ʿabd Allāh*), the highest and lowest positions that one can possibly attain.

Traditional cosmology concerns not only the macrocosm but also the microcosm. It contains a complete knowledge of the soul as it does of the qualitative aspect of the universe. As metaphysics is the key to the understanding of cosmology, so is initiation the key which opens to human beings the door to the inner chambers of their being.[14]

The cosmos is considered here to be the environment that allows human understanding to cherish God's blessings and a place for challenging the human mind to understand and unveil the physical phenomena and use them for humanity's benefit. The cosmos also allows for higher development by challenging the human soul not only to believe in the unknown, the invisible, and the absolute, but, more importantly, to submit to God, the Creator. The cosmos, with all of its multiple layers, challenges human beings to understand and realize the complexity of life and to be able to balance and harmonize the opposite forces and accept them as complementary rather than contradictory. Understanding cosmology and all of the apparently opposing forces, the physical and metaphysical, the visible and invisible, the relative and the absolute, helps to develop one's dialectical thinking. However, for believers it is the dialectics of love rather than the dialectics of war.

As human beings, we differ in our approach to relationships. Some start a relationship cautiously and with suspicion; others start with simple love and belief; yet others start with a fixed intention to use the relationship for their benefit. Some are confused and do not know what they want from that relationship, and so on. Muslims are challenged constantly to reflect, think, contemplate, and find their own way to God. From the Islamic point of view, mind and soul acquire the same knowledge by different means; at the end spirituality and intellectuality become one. Nasr argues:

> The spiritual and the intellectual are ultimately the same especially in Islamic metaphysics where *aql* in its highest sense is identified with both the Divine Intellect and the spiritual world. From the point of view of knowledge the principles of the traditional sciences are to be sought ultimately in the Divine Intellect while from the point of experience or existence they lead the traveler through the cosmic hierarchy to the spiritual world which is none other than the world of the Intellectual;

(*maʿqūlāt*, intelligibles, and *mujarradāt*, spiritual beings, are nearly synonymous in Arabic.)[15]

Thus unity and oneness are experienced from the core of the human being all the way through the cosmos and its many manifestations. A person cannot realize and experience oneness and practice it daily if she or he is split inside. In our relationships with the 'other' we as humans rarely experience the unique concept of oneness. The 'other' is mostly conceived as the 'alien' and the 'outsider,' no matter what the relationship. It can be a teacher–student, doctor–patient, employer–employee, husband–wife, and God–human or human nature relationship.

To conclude: most institutions have emerged from theories of knowledge that are split, one-sided, and unidimensional. When the West evolved into the separation of the church from the state, it consciously and deliberately separated mind from soul. Accordingly universities created scientific, educational, psychological, and sociological theories congruent with Western reductionist epistemology.

Western epistemology consciously denies one important dimension of the self, that is, the soul. The soul, many Westerners believe, is an invisible, private matter, and individuals interested in that part of their being can go to the church. So acknowledging and disciplining the soul are left to chance as an extracurricular activity. Unfortunately, the Western educational system has been exported all over the world and planted in societies that have a completely different culture and different philosophical, historical, religious, and social structure. Therefore, human beings who want to be whole persons and to accept their minds, souls, and bodies have to be aware of the concept of the One and the many. Since the One is manifested in many different ways and forms, it is left to us to realize oneness in multiplicity. This cannot be achieved from the outside in. It is an inside–out realization.

IV

TRANSFORMATION
THROUGH EDUCATION

CHAPTER EIGHT

Transformative Research Methods: An Islamic Perspective

Transformation inquiry is proposed in this book as an alternative research method that emerges from the Islamic paradigm and leads to the creation of Islamic science on one hand and inner self-transformation on the other. Bearing in mind this union of the inner experiences of the awakening of the soul from the inside and the unfolding of research experiences and knowledge from the outside, I shall begin to look at transformative research methods.

Being concerned about the knowledge produced by Muslim scholars and thousands of graduate students at Western universities, I propose using research methods that are open, yet rooted in the Islamic paradigm and the essence of *tawḥīd* (oneness and unity). The Islamic communities in Western societies are deprived of knowledge that is genuinely Islamic and contemporary at the same time. Apart from some creative and serious work produced by Muslim scholars and thinkers in the West, the Islamic academic world at Western universities is far behind what one would expect. Thousands of Muslim students have been registering at and graduating from universities in North America and Europe for decades, yet their contribution to the advan-cement of Islamic knowledge is very small. The majority of our students are choosing for their theses topics that have no relevance to Islamic issues and therefore do not contribute to the development and growth of Islamic knowledge. Moreover, by avoiding Islamic topics for their research, students are denying the development of their inner selves. The result is advanced intellectual development yet immature spiritual development. As discussed earlier, positivism in the West has created fragmented knowledge with its epistemology and quantitative research methods. Mainstream professionals and academicians in all fields have created this knowledge. Despite the fact that their view is a radically erroneous one, they form an influential proportion of the academic population.

Their view is erroneous because positivists tend to believe that reality is 'outside' themselves: that it is not only objective but also concrete and quantifiable. That is, they believe that they can stand totally outside what is real, be neutral toward it, and be able to compartmentalize, measure, and quantify it. They pride themselves on adopting scientific methods to study, control, and understand reality. What makes their method scientific, they claim, is the objective approach to reality. It is their belief that what is not quantifiable is less than real, merely subjective. Owing to positivist indoctrination at universities, Muslim students, like other students, are following the mainstream as an easy and safe passage to their graduation. By doing so, students waste the most precious years of their lives doing research that neither advances Islamic knowledge nor increases self-awareness and the awakening of the soul. Positivism, like a sharp knife, cuts apart the soul and the mind. According to positivists, what is known and researched by the mind cannot be known and sought by the soul. They maintain the position that what is not tangible and visible is not worth researching and studying. It simply does not exist for them. So Muslim students are torn between the development of the mind and that of the soul. They are indirectly made to choose between the sacred that lies inside them – invisible, silent, and profound – and the secular, aggressive demands of the modern mind. The rationale is that they have to be practical and worldly. The more they feel fragmented, the more they feel the pain of separation from their inner selves. As explained earlier, disenchantment with positivism prepared the ground for the emergence of constructivism/interpretivism. Yet both positivist and constructivist paradigms are fragmented, each in its own way. Positivism fragments human beings and knowledge into mind and soul, and deals with the mind only, ignoring the soul. Constructivism fragments reality and reduces it to a 'this-world' reality. That is to say, constructivists believe that the nature of reality is relative, and so there is no objective reality out there; nothing is absolute, everything is this-relative and hence this-worldly. Both views are reductionist, although constructivism reduces the scope of fragmentation, thus allowing for humanistic methods of inquiry.

It is important at this point to emphasize the concept of transformative inquiry and its ability to produce Islamic knowledge. The potential, however, is not solely in the inquiry method. It is the integration of transformative inquiry and the Islamic paradigm that allows for the production of Islamic science. Transformative inquiry, if used within the Islamic paradigm, can reduce the fragmentation of knowledge and self and produce holistic Islamic knowledge. My concern, as mentioned before, is twofold: (1) the production of holistic Islamic knowledge that is suitable for the Muslim community in North America and Europe; (2) the connection of students to their souls and their inner selves by transformative inquiry methods and dialectical thinking. By doing so, I hope that Muslim academicians and scholars will contribute to the faded Islamic civilization and the world's literature a knowledge that is both whole and holy. Wholeness can be achieved by producing holistic knowledge, and holiness by connecting to our inner selves and acknowledging the sacred inside us.

The concept of transformation is not a novel one; what is new is the reclaiming of the role of the sacred and the spiritual in research and inquiry. There appears to be a current need and opportunity within the scholarly domain to explore the spiritual dimension of one's life and work. It is, no doubt, an inquiry that is fraught with difficulties, complexities, and confusion. I must admit that, despite the deficiencies in the constructivist and interpretivist paradigm, it is through this open paradigm that issues related to the heart and the soul have started to leak out and become acceptable, since the main assumption of the constructivists is that the nature of reality is relative. That has been taken by some researchers to mean that anything goes, as long as it is not restricted by positivism and its assumptions of reality. I consider constructivism to be the back door into transformative inquiry that might lead to spirituality if used in the right context. It was mentioned earlier that transformative inquiry is a higher stage of development in research methods that emerge naturally and organically from the Islamic paradigm. Such an approach to inquiry has also arisen in other contexts. As methods are evolving from one level to higher levels, transformative research methods might too evolve to higher levels of development and be replaced by yet other more comprehensive methods.

The idea of transformative inquiry is not a novelty for me. I developed this idea in my doctoral thesis in 1990, and others have proposed transformative and dialectical approaches as well. I believe that hermeneutics, heuristics, phenomenology, narrative, and other qualitative research methods can be categorized as transformative inquiry. The idea of integrating qualitative research methods and the Islamic paradigm was further developed within the context of a quantum worldview and presented at the twelfth International Human Science Research (IHSR) conference at the University of Groningen in The Netherlands in 1993: the paper was titled 'Personal and Social Transformation through Transformational Research Method and Quantum Worldview.' I borrowed from the quantum worldview the two major principles of complementarity and uncertainty to present to a Western audience my ideas of transformative research methods through a holistic Islamic worldview. In this section the focus is on the concept of transformation and its relationship with research methods that I have labeled as closed and open systems. Closed systems, such as positivism, prevent transformation, whereas open systems, such as constructivism, promote transformation. However, it is argued here that neither system is appropriate for the production of Islamic knowledge. This is presented in detail in the following sections.

The transformational perspective is holistic and relational, since it emphasizes viewing the world from a complementary perspective that accommodates and accepts extremes, for they are part of reality. An important point in transformation is that the researcher adopts a holistic paradigm, a paradigm that holds as its basic premise that reality is ideal and relative, subjective and objective, spiritual and material. Holding such an open and wide perspective encourages interaction and relationships between contradictory elements. An attempt is made here to show that the transformational perspective is rooted in the Islamic worldview.

> An understanding of the world hinges on understanding the way unconscious energy mobilizes a relationship between self and situation. Human knowledge is a direct product of the process through

which humans engage and act in their world; it expresses a relationship between internal and external, subjective and objective. Tradi-
tionally, social science has sought for a knowledge emphasizing one
or another extreme in this relationship...The transformational perspective suggests that it is necessary to bridge the gap between these
extremes and ground knowledge in an understanding of the way the
internal worlds of ideas and ideals (or in the jargon of analytical psychology, of archetypes) is linked to the external world of matter.[1]

Transformation is stressed in this chapter because it indicates a
change in kind rather than degree. Transformation is defined by
Williams as "a process of human development.[2] It has as its under-
girding thought process, the theory of dissipative structures and shifts
in kind rather than degree...a difference that makes a difference a difference." So transformation indicates inclusive change or a reconstruction. Transformation occurs when the system is open and has dissipative structures (Prigogine), where elements, ideas, thoughts, and
feelings flow freely, consciously and unconsciously. The theory of
dissipative structures "is relevant to everyday life-people. It offers a
scientific model of transformation at every level."[3]

DISSIPATIVE STRUCTURES AND TRANSFORMATION

The theory of dissipative structures won the 1977 Nobel prize in
chemistry for a Belgian physical chemist, Ilya Prigogine. It explains the
"irreversible processes" in nature – the movement toward higher and
higher orders of life.

> Prigogine's theory resolves the fundamental riddle of how living things
> have been running uphill in the universe that is supposed to be running
> down...It explains the critical role of stress in transformation and the
> impetus toward transformation inherent in nature...A dissipative
> structure might well be described as flowing wholeness.[4]

Stress and tension play an important role in transformation and in
open systems, or as termed by Prigogine, 'dissipative structures.'
Instability is the key to transformation. "The dissipation of energy
creates the potential for sudden reordering."[5] Ferguson explains how
the concept of dissipative structures can be seen in human society.

The greater the instability and variation of the society, the more interactions occur. We are transformed through interaction with the environment and the situation we are studying. If the research methods we are using are open and allow for free and powerful interaction between the researcher and participants or the researcher and situation she or he is studying, then transfer of energy is possible and transformation is more likely to happen.

To go back to the concepts of change and transformation, Ferguson proposes four ways in which we change when we receive new and conflicting information.[6] These are: *change by exception*; *incremental change*; *pendulum change*; and *paradigm change*. *Change by exception* is the most limited way of changing, where our old belief system remains intact but allows for a handful of anomalies. *Incremental change* occurs gradually and the individual is not aware of having changed. *Pendulum change* fails to integrate what was right with the old and fails to discriminate the value of the new from its overstatements. Pendulum change rejects its own experience, going from one kind of half-known to another. Change in these three ways does not lead to transformation. The brain cannot deal with conflicting pieces of information unless it can integrate them or accept them through a dialectical way of thinking.

The fourth way of change suggested by Ferguson is the *paradigm change*.

> The paradigm change-transformation is the fourth dimension of change. The new perspective, the insight that allows the information to come together in a new form of structure. Paradigm change refines and integrates. Paradigm change attempts to heal the delusion of either–or, of this–or–that.[7]

Thus transformation within dissipative structures happens holistically and dialectically. It embraces the individual and society. It touches the individual and the collective consciousness.

POSITIVISM AS A CLOSED SYSTEM

Being familiar with both positivism and constructivism, we are now able to proceed to examine both paradigms from the transformative perspective. First, I shall start with the positivist paradigm as a closed system. All of the limitations imposed by the paradigm on the researcher and consequently by the research on the problem, the data, and design prevent the positivist paradigm and research methods from being an open and transformative system. A controlled and manipulative system allows energy to flow hierarchically and in one direction only; this consciously blocks all other directions and prevents a natural flow of energy.

Thus transformation is prevented. As a matter of fact, the situation, the problem, the data, and the design are all controlled consciously so that transformation does not occur. Since it disturbs the design, violates the roles and regulations of the predesigned model, and causes dependent and independent variables to interact, the researcher loses control over the study. So transformation is not acknowledged under the positivist paradigm because it causes instability and disturbance to the variables and to the design of the study.

Transformation occurs when the system is open and has in its design 'dissipative structures,' where elements, ideas, thoughts, and feelings flow freely, consciously and unconsciously. The positivist paradigm and research methods attached to it are closed systems that prevent the flow of energy, mainly because of the fragmented nature of both the paradigm and the methods. In fragmented, compartmentalized research methods, such as experimental design, there is no place for interaction, which, as a matter of fact, is prevented consciously and scientifically by experimental designs.

Therefore, assumptions such as a single and tangible reality, objectivity, control of variables, manipulation of data, cause-and-effect relationships, all connote lack of interaction and fragmentation of the problem studied by the researcher. Relationships suffer when there is fragmentation of knowledge since variables are controlled. Objectivity, for example, is an essential pillar of the positivist paradigm and statistical designs. The more detached the researcher from the 'subjects' of the study and from the data collected, the more reliable the findings, since interaction with the data might affect the results. This factor causes severe damage to relationships, blocks the flow of energy, and hence prevents transformation.

THE CONSTRUCTIVIST PARADIGM AS AN OPEN SYSTEM

Interpretive, naturalistic research methods are rooted in the constructivist paradigm. A thorough examination of the underlying assumptions of the constructivist paradigm and the knowledge produced by interpretive research methods and action research will reveal for the reader some transformational qualities that are inherent in such methods. The constructivist paradigm and interpretive research methods can be described cautiously as open systems that possess dissipative structures that are subjective, dialectic, and interactive. These characteristics allow for the free flow of energy in all directions. However, constructivism is too open and allows for a flow of energy in all directions with no restriction nor guidance, which might produce harmful and dangerous knowledge.

WHOLENESS, RELATIONSHIPS, AND TRANSFORMATION

Two important concepts that allow a system to be open or closed and that can embrace the rest of the qualities in both paradigms are the concepts of *wholeness* and *relationships*. Open systems accept a flow of energy in all directions and at all levels by the interaction between the inquirer (researcher) and the inquired into (the situation). A flow of conversation and open interviews promotes transformation. The fact that in the constructivist paradigm realities are multiple and that researchers are willing to listen to other realities and other opinions facilitates personal transformation.

Subjectivity in constructivism encourages open systems that allow for free interaction. "The knower and the known are interactive and inseparable."[8] In the constructivist paradigm there are no causal linkages nor cause-and-effect laws. Instead "all entities are in a state of mutual simultaneous shaping," so that it is impossible to distinguish the known from the knower. In open systems, control and manipulation are exercised less than in closed systems, for there is no hierarchy. In open systems the elements interact dialectically and human constructs are understood dialectically.

Transformative relationship is a whole that is more than the sum of its parts. It is synergistic, holistic. Like a dissipative structure, it is open to the world – a celebration and exploration, not a hiding place...To have a transformative relationship you must be open and vulnerable. Most people meet only at their peripheries...The transformative relationship is a shared journey toward meaning. The process itself is paramount and cannot be compromised.9

ISLAMIC PARADIGM AND TRANSFORMATIVE INQUIRY

Although the constructivist paradigm and interpretive research methods promote transformation at certain levels, the Islamic paradigm and transformational research methods have the capacity for more comprehensive and more coherent transformation. A holistic worldview must, in the end, draw all these levels – the personal, the social, and the spiritual – into one coherent whole. The Divine Principles of wholeness and complementarity play a crucial role in creating coherence and integration between dichotomies, at the levels of both the macrocosm and the microcosm.

The Islamic worldview transcends the dichotomy between mind and body, or between inner and outer. The creative dialogue between mind and matter is the physical basis of all creativity in the universe, including human creativity. The self experiences no dichotomy between the inner world of the mind and the outer world of matter because each gives rise to the other.

The transformational worldview transcends the dichotomy between the individual and the relationship by showing us that people can only be the individuals they are within a context. I am my relationships: my relationships to the subselves within my own self, my relationships to others, and my relationships to the world at large.

The fragmented worldview and quantitative research methods that we adopt increase the dichotomy in our consciousness and the knowledge produced by these research methods.

Ever since Plato, the West has stressed the rational and the analytic, the rules by which we form thoughts and make decisions...The cost of this has been the overlooking of another side to human knowing and experience, what might be called the intuitive side, the side that draws on wisdom, imagination, and creativity. In modern neurophysiological terms, these two sides of our mental life have been spoken of as the right brain/left brain split, and our culture as a left-brain culture. Using an equally good metaphor from quantum physics, we might speak of this situation as a particle/wave split and say that our culture has emphasized the particle aspect of the mind.[10]

To sum up, transformation in any field and at any level is possible only with an open system and dissipative structures. In this chapter, the positivist paradigm, experimental research methods, and statistical designs are regarded as closed systems that prevent transformation consciously or subconsciously. On the other hand, the constructivist paradigm and interpretive inquiry and research methods are considered too-open systems, which are not appropriate for the production of Islamic knowledge. Finally, the Islamic paradigm and transformative inquiry and research methods are considered open systems that promote and encourage transformation because of the concept of wholeness that underpins the above-mentioned paradigm.

In the following section I shall present four research methods that have the potential to be part of transformative inquiry, mainly because of the openness of the methods. Transformation occurs, I believe, when the system is open and has dissipative structures where elements, ideas, thoughts, and feelings flow freely consciously and subconsciously. Phenomenology, hermeneutics, heuristics, and narrative inquiry are presented here as open systems that allow for transformation. If they are integrated with the Islamic paradigm, they have the potential of producing Islamic knowledge.

PHENOMENOLOGY

Phenomenology is defined as "the systematic investigation of subjectivity."[11] Langeveld explains the aim of phenomenology as being the study of the world as it appears to us in and through consciousness.[12] The value of a phenomenological study is measured in terms of its power to let us come to the understanding of ourselves and the understanding of the lives of those for whom we bear pedagogical responsibility. The phenomenologist views human behavior – what people say and do – as a product of how people experience and define their world. The task of the phenomenologist and for us, the qualitative methodologists, is to capture this process of interpretation. In brief, the phenomenologist attempts to understand things from other people's point of view.

A phenomenological system has a different set of premises and consequently demands ethical restraints. The system is premised on radically different presumptions and assumptions regarding reality, the role of the researcher, the interaction and relationship between the researcher and the researched, and the possibility of a value-free science. Beginning with the premise that reality is a socially constructed entity, the phenomenologist looks in natural contexts for the ways in which individuals and groups make sense of their worlds. The collection of those intact realities or constructions, the interpretation of how those realities were constructed, and the understanding of the making of meaning are the main features of phenomenologically oriented inquiries.

Phenomenology can act as a two-edged sword. On the one hand, an open system of inquiry can be considered mind- and soul-liberating because of its opennesss to accommodate different views from all participants in the study. This process is called constructing realities, when the phenomenologist listens to participants as they are revealing and reconstructing their stories. They are definitely those participants' realities and nobody else's, and that is why phenomenology is defined as a systematic investigation into subjectivity. The danger lies not in constructing those 'realities,' but in *interpreting* them from a relativist perspective. It is here that many qualititative methods fail to create holistic knowledge. However, the problem is not in qualitative methods, phenomenology, or narrative. The problem is in the constructivist/interpretivist paradigm that is relativist, in which reality is socially constructed: that is to say, there is no belief in an objective reality 'out there.'

From an Islamic perspective, reality is holistic and one, and from the wholeness emerges the absolute and the relative, the permanent and the temporal, the good and the evil. Therefore, realities should be interpreted in the light of the Islamic essence of *tawḥīd*. That is to say, socially constructed realities have to be understood with reference to what 'ought to be' and not to the 'is.'

In thinking about reconstructing knowledge that facilitates and creates an Islamic epistemology, methods of social studies should be reconstructed first. Islamic scholars as well as Western scholars have expressed disenchantment about scientific research methods. Al-Fārūqī highlights three major shortcomings that render scientific approaches to research as inappropriate to Islamic knowledge: (1) the denial of relevance to a priori data; (2) false sense of objectivity; (3) personalist versus *ummatic* axiology.[13] He states:

> The western student of human nature and society was not in the mood to realize that not all the pertinent data of human behavior are observable by the senses and hence subject to quantification and measurement…Being spiritual, these elements are not isolable, separate from their natural carriers. Nor are they ever subject to the only measurement science knows, the quantitative. Science treated them as inexistent or irrelevant.[14]

He discusses an important feature of scientific, Western methodology that violates a crucial requirement of Islamic methodology, namely, unity of truth. In addition, al-Fārūqī explains how empathy and perception of values are themselves subjective.

> The perception of value is impossible unless the human behavior is able to move the observer. Similarly, the observer cannot be moved unless he is trained to be affected, and unless he has empathy with the object of his experience. The subject's attitude toward the data studied determines the outcome of the study. This is why the humanistic studies of western scientist are necessarily 'western' and cannot serve as models for the study of Muslims or their society.[15]

Finally, perhaps the most distinctive characteristic of Islamic methodology is the principle of the unity of truth. This principle holds that truth is a modality of God and is inseparable from Him, that truth is one just as God is One. It is invalid to seek to establish the knowledge of human reality without acknowledging what that reality ought to be. Any investigation of a human 'is' must therefore include its standing as an 'ought to be' within the realm of possibility.

An important feature of Islamic methodology and knowledge

throughout history is their wholeness. A holistic, phenomenological or naturalistic methodology could, no doubt, create integrated, unified knowledge that leads to the realization of the unity of truth. By realizing and accepting the dialectical concept of *tawḥīd*, Muslim scholars are challenged to search for truth in contradictory and opposing ideas and situations. Studying any problem phenomenologically allows the researcher to examine the situation as it reveals itself naturally without a priori conditioning. It also allows the researcher to observe the relationship between various elements as they interact in a natural setting. By doing so, the researcher is in a position to see and experience the 'whole' picture, or at least as whole as human limitations permit.

An educational problem, for example, if studied holistically or phenomenologically, reveals the interaction between the individual and the situation. Philosophically speaking, the method reveals the interaction between human beings and the universe. Scientific approaches, however, could not encompass the wholeness of problems.

> The answer to these shortcomings lies, of course, in the phenomenological method, which requires that the observer let the phenomena speak for themselves rather than force them into any predetermined ideational framework; let the eidetic vision of essence order the data for the understanding and be corroborated by them. These essentials of the phenomenological method were known to and meticulously observed by the Muslim scholar Abū al-Rayḥān al-Bīrūnī (440/1048) in his classical study of the religion and culture of India. The methodological principles he established were continued in a long tradition of comparative learning and writing by Muslims. The phenomenological method was first introduced into western philosophy by Edmund Husserl, and into the study of ethics and religion by Max Scheler.[16]

Al-Bīrūnī used phenomenology and other methods of inquiry to study and understand India and its complex and rich culture. When he started his study on India in his book, *Tahqīq mā li al-Hind,* ("Verification of What is Said on India"), al-Bīrūnī was confronted with the difficult task of how to understand a civilization with radically different customs, values, languages, and view of the world. Al-Bīrūnī was recognizing the dilemma of all interpretations of other civilizations, especially when he had his doubts about the reliability of the reports and translations that were available. So he created his own multimethods for studying other cultures.

In the fifth century AH (eleventh century AC) al-Bīrūnī used what is called today triangulation to gain an understanding of Indian civilizations. According to Chelkowski, al-Bīrūnī used three methods. First, he would let the Hindus speak for themselves in their own words.[17] "It was rather a way toward truth." Second, al-Bīrūnī undertook the painstaking task of "learning the language most suitable for gaining insight into the civilization."[18] Al-Bīrūnī's choice was Sanskrit. He chose Sanskrit so as to be able to read and analyze the written documents and to understand the roots of the culture. He wanted to know the 'ought to be' from the Hindu perspective. Al-Bīrūnī used comparative methods to understand Hindu culture and philosophy. Thirdly he compared Hindu philosophy with Greek, Sufi and Christian concepts and philosophy. He was searching for a human thread that connects all ancient cultures. Al-Bīrūnī was looking for new sources of knowledge from the Hindu culture in the same way as Greek thought and philosophy were translated and utilized by Muslim Scholars.[19]

By analyzing the multiple methods used by al-Bīrūnī in his studies of a different civilization and culture, we realize that he used qualitative research methods in his phenomenological approach. He used three major techniques for collecting the data for his study. First, he interviewed Hindus and allowed them to reveal their stories or to 'construct their realities.' Second, he studied the language of the religious texts so as to be able to read and understand the belief system from the written text and thus interpret what was said by people as they constructed their realities, to compare what 'is' with what 'ought to be' as it was written in the religious books. So the interpretation was made in the context of that civilization. Thirdly, al-Bīrūnī used comparative study methods to compare and contrast so as to understand the similarities and differences. So al-Bīrūnī employed interviewing, participant observation, document analysis, and comparative methods for his phenomenological study.

This is an illustration of how constructive/interpretive and phenomenological methods can be used effectively if guided by an Islamic worldview, a worldview that is holistic and open and does not allow for a priori misconceptions. The emphasis is always on the worldview because it is the base for all the other elements that constitute any civilization. No matter how powerful any methodology is, if it is based on a fragmented paradigm or worldview, that methodology is doomed to be fragmented and reductionist.

> It is this all-embracing emphasis on the unity of science and religion, knowledge and values, physics and metaphysics, which gives Islamic science its unique character. And it is its insistence on multiplicity of methods which gives it a characteristic style with synthesis as its main feature...As such, Islamic science is subjectively objective, that is, it seeks subjective goals within an objective framework.[20]

HEURISTIC RESEARCH

Heuristic research is another type of inquiry that I categorize as an open system and that has the potential for the transformation of both the research and the researcher. I focus in this section on the approach used by Moustakas.[21] The nature and underlying assumptions of heuristic research are such that they engage the researcher in an intense relationship so that transformation is only a natural process of such an inquiry. As researchers, we always choose the methods that are most appropriate for the nature of the questions that are asked. Moustakas focuses on the transformation of the self during the procedure of the research. The importance of heuristic research lies in its ability to engage the researcher in an intense relationship with the phenomena that she or he is studying. The phenomena under study in such an inquiry are usually deep personal experiences that had or still have a great effect on the researcher, experiences that have touched the furthest corners of her/his being. Moustakas defines heuristic research as:

> the process of internal search through which one discovers the nature and meaning of experiences and develops methods and procedures for further investigation and analysis...Heuristic processes incorporate creative self-processes and self-discoveries. In such a process not only is knowledge extended but the self of the researcher is illuminated.[22]

It is this illumination and awakening of the soul that I should like to emphasize in the academic world and in this book. Research can be empty, cold, and dispassionate if it does not touch the very core of our being. Heuristic inquiry entails self-search, self-discovery, and self-dialogue. The intensity of the experience reflects the importance of that experience to the awakening of the soul. Because of the autobiographical nature of the heuristic inquiry, the research is set on a journey to the inner self. When she or he is touched by the meeting of the soul, nothing can be the same again: it is here that the transformation occurs. Experiences take different directions and deeper meaning. Heuristic research demands the total and undivided presence of the whole person – body, mind, and soul – to enter this intense experience and "to risk the opening of wounds and passionate concerns and to undergo the personal transformation that exists as a possibility in every heuristic journey."[23]

Heuristic inquiry is a method that has the potential for engaging researchers in soul searching and the discovery of the inner self. The ultimate aim, however, is the transformation of a divided mind, body, and soul into a whole person who accepts her/his intellectual as well as her/his spiritual experiences as one unified whole. Moustakas suggests six stages through which a researcher passes to accomplish a heuristic research: (1) identifying the focus of inquiry; (2) self-dialogue; (3) tacit-knowing; (4) intuition; (5) in-dwelling; and (6) focusing.[24] Then he identifies the phases of heuristic research: (1) initial engagement; (2) immersion; (3) inculcation; (4) illumination; (5) explication; and (6) creative synthesis.[25]

> The conscious aspect of the individual consists of transformed unconscious energy…Transformation occurs as energy moves from the unconscious side of the person over to the conscious side…Another way of appreciating the significance of this process and the importance of the unconscious in social life, stems from the realization that transformation lies at the basis of meaningful action…Meaningful experience involves the discovery of capacities and potential in self and situations that have previously remained hidden.[26]

What is important, therefore, in any research is the positive energy produced by such a transformation and realization for the reconstructing of the self and the situation under study. Without such a transformation, education remains a meaningless process that has no real effect on students, teachers, and society in general. The choice of methodology determines to what extent the researcher is aware of the importance of her/his study and the knowledge that will be produced by such a methodology. Being prepared to go through the pain of creating and discovering also indicates the maturity of the researcher and the work that is going to be produced. The transformational perspective focuses on creating a dialogue between the extremes in life: the internal and the external, the subjective and the objective. The problem of the social researcher, as Morgan states, is thus "one of finding an appropriate means of linking one's self to the situation being researched."[27] Therefore, to fulfill the thesis of this book, which is promoting the production of Islamic knowledge, it is important to suggest paradigms and methods that are appropriate for its development, namely, methods that help researchers in the transformation and in relating their inner selves to the situation under study.

What are important in any methodology used are not only the techniques and protocols of that inquiry but, more importantly, the paradigm that regulates and affects the interpretation of the constructed meanings. What makes any research Islamic or non-Islamic, however, is not only the research method, but also the paradigm that leads the interpretation. No interpretation can be called Islamic if it is not rooted in the Islamic, holistic paradigm with the Divine Principles of the One and the Absolute at its center.

HERMENEUTICS

Any inquiry regarded from an Islamic perspective ought to be multidimensional and multileveled. No issue, no matter how small, is one-dimensional. Accordingly, a multidimensional problem cannot be understood and analyzed if multidimensional methods are not used. Researchers have to be open and flexible to operate within different inquiry methods so as to be able to capture the complexity of the phenomena under study. Both phenomenology and heuristic inquiry deal with personal, subjective experiences of the participants or the phenomena under study. "Hermeneutics itself is a very old type of text study that was originally confined to theological documents. The word simply means 'interpretation.' Over time, the strategies of hermeneutics have undergone various reformation."[28] Hermeneutics is much older than phenomenology, essentially a form of exegesis. It was developed for the examination of biblical texts. It is defined in dictionaries as "the art and science of interpretation." "Martin Heidegger and then Paul Ricouer masterfully appropriated hermeneutics for the social sciences by suggesting that human actions can be understood and interpreted, the same way a written text appears to the reader."[29] If we accept the idea of "reading society as a text," as suggested by R.H. Brown,[30] hermeneutics can be used as an effective tool for understanding the complexity of society and the collective action of human beings in certain situations.

> The notion of text is a good paradigm for human action...[because human action is in many ways a quasi-text...Even more like a text, of which the meaning has been freed from the initial conditions of its production..., action, like a text, is an open work, addressed to an indefinite series of possible 'reader.'[31]

Hermeneutics, therefore, deals with social issues and the collective consciousness. Social issues are as important as personal issues, if not more so, because they touch the lives of many people. Islam addresses social issues in the Divine Book and emphasizes the concept of the *ummah* (the Islamic community and nation).

> The social order is the heart of Islam, and stands prior to the personal. Indeed, Islam views the personal as a necessary prerequisite for the societal, and regards human character as warped if it rested with the personal and did not transcend it to the societal.[32]

Hermeneutics is more interested in the social than the individual meaning of actions. "Unlike phenomenology, hermeneutics is not concerned with the experienced intention of the individual, but takes action as an access through which to interpret the larger social context of meaning within which it is embedded."[33] However, like phenomenology, hemeneutics is an attempt to describe and study meaningful phenomena in a systematic, sincere, and passionate manner.

Passionate, because the researcher cannot distance herself or himself from the phenomena under study, whether engaged in hermeneutic, heuristic, or phenomenological inquiry. Within a hermeneutic approach, the relationship between the knower and the known may be a close mutual relationship of respect and empathy.

NARRATIVE AND AUTOBIOGRAPHY

We are coming to realize the power of rhetoric and narrative and dialogue for understanding ourselves and others...The telling of stories or songs of experiences if you will signals the return of the inquirer as a morally and emotionally engaged knower. We are obligated to explore how acknowledging and celebrating this engagement furthers our efforts to interpret ourselves to ourselves.34

Narrative inquiry is another complementary method in the multi-method approach to research that gained momentum in the 1980s and 1990s.35 Like several other qualitative research methods, narrative inquiry has the potential to create holistic knowledge if it is rooted in a holistic paradigm. However, if narrative is rooted in one-dimensional paradigms like the interpretivist/constructivist, where the nature of reality is relative and there is no absolute, objective reality, or if it is guided by idealists/positivists, where the nature of reality is absolute and singular, even if applied to temporary situations and daily life, then the knowledge produced will be one-dimensional and will not contribute to the production of holistic knowledge. Since reality is both relative and absolute, this-worldly and other-worldly, subjective and objective, it is only common sense that the methodologies employed must be of sufficient power and sophistication to understand and interpret these complexities. No one methodology has yet been discovered that is able to do so. Therefore, multiple methods for the present time may construe a trustworthy approach to use.

Research and thinking are always based on personal concerns. Even when the issues that preoccupy us are mainly social, political, or spiritual, or affect humanity in general, there are always highly personal reasons why these more universal issues mean so much to us. What is certainly true is that we researchers trust certain methods of research and reflection because they have made sense to us, because they have shed light on issues that are personally important to us, possibly even because they are related to important events of childhood. Stories prove that much more is hidden in our lives than we at first realize. We have to learn to take our own experiences seriously. My reflection on personal experiences has persuaded me that, hidden in our lives, are resources for understanding and interpretation. Contact with our own life story is for us a way to self-discovery, self-dialogue, and self-knowledge, and beyond that is an entry to our souls and our spirituality. No matter what the internal phenomena are that we are trying to understand, as long as they are inside us and we risk opening old wounds, that journey puts us in touch with our real selves, our souls.

> Seeking knowledge within the self or seeking the meaning of one's life can be the hardest riddle or koan of all. Each of us is unique and the journey inward leads us through the blind spots of our own vision. Yet, we know the way; we have come from there.[36]

Narrative inquiry, if practiced within an Islamic paradigm, can illuminate the soul and awaken the inner self because of its inherent qualities of intimacy and courage. Such an inquiry entails the difficult task of entering one's own soul and subconscious. Yet doing so gives us the courage to create and reconstruct our personal experiences, to go beyond the pain and the hurt, and transform the pain into higher qualities of acceptance, understanding, and submission to God's will. Narrative inquiry can be the first step on the long spiritual journey, where we are in continual dialogue with our inner self, God, and the 'other.'

CHAPTER NINE

Transformative Learning

METHODS FOR HOLISTIC EDUCATION

Holistic methods that are congruent with holistic principles for education are proposed in this chapter. Based on the profundity of Islamic teaching and the high position granted to human beings, these methods propose a holistic development of human abilities, physical, intellectual, and spiritual. Developing students' abilities holistically enhances their integrity and empowers them to face the challenges of life. The development is gradual, yet directed and purposeful, with steps leading to higher and yet higher levels of perfection. Material development and material gains are considered only as the basic requirement for human and societal development. Thus the holistic methods cater to all aspects of individual and societal improvement.

The three methods proposed for such a development are (1) dialectical thinking; (2) reflection and meditation; (3) conversation and dialogue. An overview of the approaches is briefly presented here, followed by a separate and more detailed explanation of each one.

The first approach is dialectical thinking that will help students to develop their intellectual abilities, and thus establish intellectual connectedness. Simply put, it will establish the body–mind connection. In their educational experience, many Muslim students in the West feel a spiritual vacuum that needs to be addressed properly to fulfill the need of wholeness. Students are disconnected from their inner selves and from their rich Islamic heritage. We all know that knowing the self leads to knowing God. To reconnect students with their selves, several methods are described. Second, reflection and meditation are proposed as practical methods for connecting students with their experiences and their inner selves. Spiritual connectedness can be achieved by this step where body, mind, and soul are unified, and the individual feels that she or he is a whole person. It must be mentioned that no clear-cut division exists between the various faculties; the categorization here is to clarify the ideas of connectedness.

The third approach to unifying people with their inner selves and their surroundings is to promote understanding with the 'other' and others with hermeneutic methods as well as with conversation. In this way, communication and dialogue are established between individuals in society, between parents and children, between teachers and students, and so on. This helps students to unify the polarization in the community and encourages communications at the university among colleagues from other religions and other nationalities. In the process, a connection is established between the whole person and the unified society.

DIALECTICAL THINKING

Dialectical thinking is discussed here at two levels: (1) as a method for transformation; (2) as the highest stage of faith development. The questions in this book are embedded in dialectics and interpreted by dialectical analysis. Issues of social and personal development can be best presented, understood, analyzed and interpreted by using dialectical theories. Most Western literature on dialectics deals with this issue from a philosophical or psychological perspective; in the East, there is the philosophical and theological perspective in Islamic literature. This book attempts to synthesize dialectical theories of development and proposes dialectical thinking as a method that, if practiced within the Islamic paradigm, can lead to the path of *tawḥīd*. This dialectics will be referred to as 'the dialectics of *tawḥīd*.' I am aware that the very term 'dialectics of *tawḥīd*' may appear contradictory but what is meant here is the dialectics that leads to *tawḥīd* and unity instead of wars and arguments.

DIALECTICAL THINKING AND TRANSFORMATION

The writings of Klaus Riegel,[1] Michel Basseches,[2] and James Fowler[3] on dialectical theory and faith development are major sources in this chapter. A brief review of the dialectical theory is now presented. Basseches asserts:

Dialectical thinking as an intellectual tradition represents a third alternative to two powerful styles of thought which have exerted considerable influence on contemporary humanistic, scientific, and social thought, in both their professional and their 'common sense' forms. I call these styles universalistic formal thinking and realistic thinking.[4]

Dialectical thinking as an alternative school of thought comprises a family of worldviews of the nature of existence (ontology) and knowledge (epistemology). "These apparently contradictory worldviews share a family of resemblance based on three features – *common emphases on change, wholeness and internal relations.*"[5]

The concepts of (1) *change*; (2) *wholeness*; and (3) *internal relations* are basic assumptions in dialectical thinking. Transformation happens when these three elements interact and transform contradictions to complementarity, fragments to wholeness, and the many to the One. The internal relations are essential in dialectical thinking. It is from the interaction of contradictions that we as human beings realize the whole. A dialectical worldview answers the questions of ontology, or "what exists by assuming fundamental ongoing processes of change or of becoming, in which old forms give way to new emergent forms." In addition to the idea of change, a dialectical worldview emphasizes wholeness in two ways:

First, conceptualizing entities as forms of existence rather than as elements of existence emphasizes the sense of coherence, organization and wholeness implicit in the notion of forms as against the sense of separateness implicit in the notion of element. Secondly, since these forms are viewed as temporary rather than as immutable, the entities themselves are de-emphasized relative to the process of existence as a whole which is viewed as characterized by continual differentiation and integration.[6]

Internal relations are an important conceptual feature of the dialectical worldview.

The relations among parts within a whole help make the parts what they are, and thus the relations are 'internal' to the nature of the parts. At the same time, the relations form the internal structure of the whole.[7]

Basseches defines dialectic as follows: "Dialectic is development transformation (i.e., *developmental movement through forms*) *which occurs via constitutive and interactive relationship*."[8]

Accepting the idea of wholeness simply means accepting the challenge of contradictions that are inherent in wholeness, and hence accepting contradictions in daily life. Riegel, in his dialectical theory of development, proposes a final stage of cognitive development, namely dialectical operations. At this stage the individual

> is able to accept contradictions as the basis of all thought and to tolerate conflicting operations without equilibrating their order in all circumstances. In applying the notion of dialectical operations to the present interpretations, the individual becomes not only able to tolerate contradictions in different developmental progressions, i.e., those that are brought about by lack of coordination, but he seeks these as constructive confrontations and accepts them as the basis for all development and operations. Subsequently the dialectical individual does not experience asynchronies as crises or catastrophes but regards them as essential and constructive steps through which alone developmental progression becomes possible.[9]

Accepting contradictions is an important stage of dialectical thinking that can enrich one's experiences and enhance both personal adult development and social development. This leads to another level of interaction in dialectical theory: the inner dialectics and the outer dialectics that were recognized by Riegel.[10]

A dialectical theory must embrace both inner dialectics (intrapersonal), expressed, for example, in Piaget's concepts of assimilation and accommodation within the cognitive development of the active individual, and outer (interpersonal) dialectics, concerned with the social and physical interactions of different individuals who are simultaneously engaged in their own active change and development. Inner dialectics and outer dialectics are interdependent; thus transformation occurs when the individual moves beyond the consideration of either one of these interactive processes in isolation and arrives at a concept of the complex interaction of both. This expanded concept of dialectics places the human being at the intersection of interaction. The changing events within individuals interact with and influence the changing events in the outer world of which they are a part. Conversely, the changing events in the outer world are influencing the changing events within the individual.

DIALECTICAL THINKING AND FAITH DEVELOPMENT

In addition to its ability to develop one's intellectual thinking, dialectical thinking has the power of spiritual development, which is discussed here. Dialectical thinking has been recognized as the highest stage of personal development by several psychologists in the West, including Fowler,[11] Broughton,[12] Riegel,[13] and Basseches.[14] Fowler associated dialectical thinking with faith development, and his theory is presented below.[15]

Fowler's investigation into faith development identified six sequential stages, the fifth and sixth of which are exclusively the phenomena of adult development. Fowler called stage 5 'conjunctive faith.'

> This stage affirms and incorporates logical polarities, acting on a felt need to hold them in tension in the interest of truth...It is not simply relativist, affirming that one person's faith is as good as another's as if equally strongly held. It holds its vision with a kind of provisional ultimacy.[16]

Faith developed from the dialectics of *tawḥīd* is the cornerstone for self-development in Islam. Inheriting one's religion does not necessarily mean having faith in that religion. It is like inheriting the family name. Faith requires cultivation and devotion to the quest, as in developing one's thinking ability. Individuals gradually develop their own awareness of their faith and the worldview on which they build their faith and their lives. From an Islamic point of view, development includes a believer's faith in God, the prophets, the angels, the hereafter, and the Day of Judgment. Faith in these will eventually lead to the right path. For this reason, the higher education system should include the development of the students' faith in its curricula. Faith, like dialectical thinking, develops gradually with maturity. The deliberate development of students' dialectical thinking and faith guides them on to the straight path of Islam.

Alive to paradox and truth in the apparent contradictions, this stage strives to unify opposites in mind and experience. It generates and maintains vulnerability to the strange truths of those who are 'other.' Ready for closeness to that which is different and threatening to self and outlook…But this stage remains divided. It lives and acts between an untransformed world and transforming vision and loyalties.[17]

The dialectics that leads to the path of *tawḥīd* and its underlying principles of unity is a powerful tool that Islam provides for its followers to understand paradoxical situations and to be able to develop a strong faith in the Absolute One. The dialectics of *tawḥīd* helps individuals to realize the Principle of Divine Unity that underlies the apparent paradox in what Fowler calls "an untransformed world and a transforming vision and loyalties."

Growth and development are fundamental concerns of Islam. Evolution from the lower to the higher, from the physical to the spiritual, is a natural process in the development of humans. As human beings climb the ladder of self-development and self-awareness, they become more open-minded and more willing to release themselves from old ideas, habits, and established loyalties to certain schools of thought. Dialectical thinking gradually lets go of the clinging grip of habit for the sake of realizing the Truth. It helps human beings to evolve gradually and naturally by realizing the truth in their inner being.

A man is deficient in understanding until he perceives that there is a whole cycle of evolution possible within himself: Repeating endlessly, offering opportunities for personal development.[18]

Thus the dialectics of *tawḥīd* leads the individual to the highest stages of personal development by realizing the potential intellect and the inner mysteries of the self and by coming to the realization of God and the essence of Divine Unity. Individuals at stage 5 remain paradoxical and divided as they move to stage 6 of faith development. The tension between stability and change is transcended in stage 6 by a complete sacrifice of the former for the latter. As Fowler describes it, achievement of this stage is much more a matter of grace than of psychological development. Nevertheless, because this stage is an outgrowth of the tensions of stage 5, both depend on the development of dialectical thinking and go beyond it.

The self at Stage 6 engages in spending and being spent for the transformation of present reality in the direction of a transcendent actuality. Persons best described by Stage 6 typically exhibit qualities that
shake our usual criteria of normalcy. Their heedlessness to self-preser-
vation and the vividness of their taste and feel for transcendent moral
and religious actuality give their actions and words an extraordinary
and often unpredictable quality...It is little wonder that persons best
described by Stage 6 so frequently become martyrs for the visions they
incarnate.[19]

Dialectical thinking is a powerful tool for both intellectual and
spiritual development if used within the Islamic paradigm. It can promote an Islamic holistic knowledge and contribute to building healthy
minds and souls capable of surviving the aggression of the modern
age.

AWAKENING OF THE SOUL

The second method in holistic education is geared toward developing
students' spirituality and inner power by daily ritual prayers, meditation, and reflection. Such approaches touch the inner depth of the soul
and the mind. The awakening of the soul leads to self-realization and
thus realization of the unity of the Divine Principle.

As a perceptive and rational being, he [the human being] is intended to
reach full awareness of his essential nature. He is to become effective in
his life. Education, therefore, is the treatment of man as a creature who
is developing an awareness and understanding of himself. It should sti-
mulate him to this understanding and show him how to achieve it.[20]

RITUAL PRAYERS

The path of transformation begins within. By renewing ourselves in
daily prayers and meditation, we discover a deep source of inner peace
which creates a deeper peace around us. We can transform our world
by transforming our attitude. This cannot be accomplished by merely
reading or thinking about inner peace, love, and eternal happiness.
Living the path is more than an intellectual exercise. The serenity
gained from meeting and acknowledging the sacred inside us creates

inner and outer peace; it helps to keep one's life in order. Balanced, responsible, and at peace with oneself, one radiates peace to all one meets. Cultivating that inner peace and reclaiming the sacred inside us to make us whole and sometimes holy. We become whole when we acknowledge both our intellect and spirit as one unified entity so that we are not divided between our minds and our souls. We consider not only the material benefits of any action performed, but more importantly its spiritual benefits and to what extent it pleases God.

One of the five pillars of Islam is the salah to be performed five times a day at prescribed hours between the moment before sunrise and the beginning of complete darkness. Early Muslim mystics regarded ritual prayers as a kind of ascension to heaven, as a *mi'rāj* that brought them into the immediate presence of God. "The connection of the *mi'rāj* with daily prayer – which was experienced by Muhammad as a repetition of the joy of ascension – made such an ascension into the divine presence possible for every sincere Muslim."[21]

From an Islamic point of view, purification of the soul and the heart underlies all religious rites. All rituals in Islam have an extrinsic and intrinsic significance, the former for societal development, the latter for individual development. The inner meaning of prayer, pilgrimage, fasting, alms giving, and jihad fosters spirituality and the awakening of the soul. A common image used in Islam for the effect of purifying the soul and receiving intuitive bliss is that of the mirror. Islamic rites cleanse the mirror of the soul from the dust of sin and prepare it to receive the Divine Truth; this internal prayer purifies the heart.

> Shaykh 'Abd al-Qādir Jīlānī called this internal prayer the prayer of the path (*ṣalāt al-ṭarīqah*) and described it in the following way: "its mosque is the *qalb* (heart). Its congregation is the conglomeration of all internal forces in man. It recites with spiritual tongue the names of God's unity (*tawḥīd*). Its imam is a deep spiritual urge in the heart (*al-shawq fīl-fu'ād*). Its qibla (direction of prayer) is the unity of the Godhead (*aḥadiyyah*). The *qalb* (heart) and *rūḥ* (spirit) are constantly engaged in this prayer. They neither sleep, nor do they die."[22]

The fostering of prayers in a holistic education is important because this helps students to attain self-connectedness by using methods which they know – such as Islamic rites – but which have been practiced so mechanically that their inner, spiritual meaning has been lost.

REFLECTION

Reflection on God's creation, the cosmos, and the universe is a method that is related to praying. In this context, it connects students with their inner selves and their personal experiences.

> They know the outward of this world's life, but of the hereafter they are heedless. Do they not reflect within themselves? Allah did not create the heavens and the earth and what is in between them but with truth, and [for] an appointed term. And surely most of the people are deniers of the meeting with their Lord. (The Qur'an, 30:7, 8)

The purpose of reflection is twofold. First, it enhances students' spirituality by connecting them to their inner being so as to understand and know themselves and discover their inner potential, all of which will become apparent in their education and their lives. Second, reflection helps students to transcend their knowledge of themselves, bringing them to the knowledge of the unity of the Natural and the Divine Principle helping them to go beyond realization and experience oneness, the concept of *tawḥīd*, the ultimate goal of Islam. Reflection and meditation are intimately related, so they can be used interchangeably. The importance of reflection lies in its unifying nature that connects the person to her or his experience and then transcends that experience to higher levels. This chapter has demonstrated how human beings evolve gradually from self-realization to the realization of the unity of God's knowledge. Islam is a developmental school of thought that eventually transcends the material to attain the spiritual.

> The Divine Oneness implies not only transcendence but also immanence. The Qur'an asserts over and over again the transcendence of God above and beyond all categories of human thought and imagination.... Islamic spirituality is based on the constant awareness of this transcendence, of the impotence of all things before His Power and the perishable nature of all existence in contrast to His ever-living and eternal Nature.[23]

So, prayer and meditation will help students to realize the concept of transcendence of the Divine Oneness. It will help them to experience transcendence at personal levels and to realize that God is beyond and above all creations.

THE ART OF CONVERSATION: CONNECTING TO THE 'OTHER'

Disconnection with oneself and one's inner being surely causes separation from other people and society in general. The spiritual and intellectual disconnectedness in Muslim communities at all levels fragments people's experiences and alienates them from their inner being and from society. People who are not taught how to communicate with themselves are not able to communicate with others naturally and intelligently. The depth of our conversations reveals the degree of our connectedness to our inner powers. The superficial talk that prevails in society indicates a high level of disconnectedness.

The following section presents a means of developing community connectedness in Muslim society. Its aim is to improve communication and dialogue between individuals and Muslim communities inside and outside the university.

Using the art of conversation as a method to develop students' abilities can have a therapeutic effect on both the individual and society. Students will be taught how to converse and express their views without being caught up in their prejudices. Conversation can be relaxing, loose, and enjoyable, or it can be challenging and require techniques for presenting ideas. So, developing students' conversational abilities under the supervision of a dialectical teacher trains students in the principles of discussion, presenting ideas, arguing, agreeing, disagreeing, and debating. Lack of dialogical skills can, unintentionally, cause severe problems. Dialogue, like any other skill, requires understanding and practice.

DIALOGUE AS A MEANS OF CONNECTION

Dialogue and conversation are used interchangeably in this section to refer to the ability to exchange ideas and views verbally. Dialogue is a commonplace method proposed in the context of wholeness and unity of self, knowledge, and community. Dialogue is one of the powerful modes of communicating and building relationships. It needs neither advanced technology and expensive equipment nor complicated techniques. Dialogue is an art in itself. Some people are conversationalists by nature. Learning how to listen and empathize with others is the first step. The next step is to be open to what the other wants to say, and enter into the thoughts and feelings of the other person. However, it is the sincerity and personal character of the people engaged in the conversation that determine its quality and depth. Home, school, and university are ideal places for developing a person's manners and ability to converse and to listen.

At universities the situation is such that students are either overloaded with assignments, or they are distracted with the trivialities of modern life so that they hardly have time for real dialogue or intellectual or spiritual conversation. The pace of life neither allows nor leads one to appreciate a few hours of reflection or conversation. Students at university often do not have much opportunity to engage in intelligent conversation. They do not develop this God-given gift of speech as a discourse. So schools and universities should be the obvious places to help students develop the art and skill of conversation.

The power of conversation lies in its wholeness as a means of communication. Communication in this mode is not restricted to the mind, body, or soul. It is a dynamic interaction between two or more 'wholes.' These wholes communicate thoughts, feelings, hopes, and aspirations. A powerful genuine conversation unites the past, present, and future in one small incident. No other tool possesses the flexibility and immediacy of conversation. A powerful conversation is a dialectical conversation. It is like the dialectics of the sea and the sand on the Arabian shores. The conversation between the sea and the sand is powerful, despite the striking differences between the substance of each one. The waves penetrate the sands and the water sinks between the grains. The sand accepts the invitation for a deeper and higher level and moves with the waves away from the periphery to the center where the meeting of the mind and the soul reaches fulfillment. However, some controversial issues in life cannot be understood and accepted even from dialectical conversation. These issues remain unsolved forever.

In brief, this chapter has proposed three methods of developing and promoting holistic education. These are considered options complementary to the existing methods of teaching at universities in order to heal the friction caused by fragmented education systems. Thus the common theme throughout these three holistic methods is connectedness and unity. First, connection with the mind can be gained by developing dialectical thinking. Second, connection with the inner self can be regained by using spiritual methods such as daily ritual prayers, meditation, and reflection. This leads to self-knowledge and new personal experiences which, in turn, lead to connection with God, nature, and the universe as a silent type of connection.

Third, connection between the individual and society can be created by communication and conversation. Dialogue and conversation help to open channels for communication between different groups. In addition, conversation with oneself builds a bridge between opposing ideas. This is an active, not a silent type of self-connection. It is hoped that Muslim students in North America and Europe utilize the unique opportunity that they enjoy of having the best of both worlds. They have an Islamic background and Western research facilities that allow them the freedom to pursue research and to develop knowledge that is based on Islamic epistemology and that represents the Islamic holistic paradigm. Other methods of research and learning are proposed to our graduate and undergraduate students to help them acquire qualities of wholeness and holiness so that they can contribute to the development of Islamic sacred science.

To sum up, education has been suffering from unidimensionality at all levels for a long time in schools and universities in the East and the West. Being scientific and rational is the key to success in schooling and in life in general. The human being is regarded as mind and body only and that is reflected in the education system. Intellectuality and rationality are reinforced and encouraged, whereas spirituality and intuition are downplayed and ignored. The ultimate goal of life is being reduced to achieving worldly and material objectives. The goal of purifying the soul to attain the ultimate truth and the hereafter is being ignored in education and in life generally.

This book is an attempt to restore wholeness and holiness to education, using transformative learning and teaching methods. It also proposes other paradigms that lead to the Islamic theory of knowledge as a first step in producing Islamic knowledge based on the Islamic paradigm and emerging from Islamic epistemology. An attempt has been made to present epistemology from an educational rather than a philosophical point of view. Having been a teacher for a long time in school and at university, I much prefer to address philosophical issues at a practical level, allowing students to examine the roots of the knowledge that they are acquiring and the knowledge that they are producing later in graduate schools and as researchers. Fragmentation of knowledge and therefore of the self exists in all circles consciously and/or subconsciously. Philosophical questions are an essential part that exists within us from an early age. If they are not addressed at that early age, then we are planting the seeds of fragmentation. So education has to be rooted in philosophical issues and students should be aware of that philosophical base to be able to see the roots of what they are learning. Without such awareness, what students learn does not exceed their academic record and celebration of their graduation. The transformation perspective is proposed in this book as a means of creating Islamic knowledge. A knowledge that is meaningful to Muslim students and scholars, because transformation lies at the basis of meaningful action as Morgan says.[24] Transformation has been proved to be an irreversible flow upwards in the scale of being.

What intrigues me is that both Ṣadr al-Mutalihīn al-Shīrāzī, who is also known as Mullā Ṣadrā, the sixteenth-century Muslim philosopher, and the twentieth-century Belgian physical chemist, Ilya Prigogine, the winner of the Nobel prize in 1977 for his theory of dissipative structures and the 'irreversible processes,' reached the same conclusion, one from a philosophical perspective and the other from a purely scientific perspective. Prigogine explains in detail his theory of dissipative structures and how living things have been running uphill in the universe.[25] He also explains the inherent transformative nature of living things and the movement to a more complex and perfect thing. The paradox in this theory is an intriguing one. The more coherent the structure, the more unstable it is. This very instability is the key to transformation. The dissipation of energy, as Prigogine demonstrated mathematically, creates the potential of sudden reordering.

Mullā Ṣadrā, on the other hand, explains the transformation and perfection of the body–soul complex as follows:

> Movement-in-substance is not universal change or flux without direction, the product of conflict between two equally powerful principles, or a reflection of the non-being of the world of nature when measured against the world of permanent forms. It is rather the natural beings' innate desire to become more perfect, which directs this ceaseless self renewal, self origination, or self-emergence into a perpetual and irreversible flow upward in the scale of being – from the simplest elements to the human body–soul complex and the heavenly body–soul complex (both of which participate in the general instability, origination, and passing of being that characterizes the entire corporeal world. The human body–soul complex and the heavenly body–soul complex are not moved externally by the Intelligences. Their movement is an extension of the process of self-perfection. Having reached the highest rank of order of substance, in the corporeal world, they are now prepared, and still moved by their innate desire, to flow upward and transform themselves into pure intelligence.[26]

This quotation opens new avenues for another book to look into transformation in more depth and to relate philosophical concepts and scientific research of applied sciences to understand in a practical way the relationship of the microcosm and macrocosm.

APPENDIX

THE ERUPTION OF THE VOLCANO

The following is a reflection on my experiences as a doctoral student at the University of Toronto. The accumulation of many diverse and conflicting experiences in the East and the West created a volcano within me that lay dormant for many years and then was suddenly activated into eruption. No one particular factor can be pinpointed as the cause for the eruption. I believe that the dynamic clash and interaction of accumulated conflicting experiences can create unexplainable phenomena inside a person. When those internal phenomena are pressured, hammered, or even touched by an intellectual challenge or a spiritual spark, an eruption occurs. It might cause destruction—but it leaves rich, fertile soil behind. Maybe philosophers would call this "synthesis" arising from the dialectic of the thesis and antithesis. Since I believed in the intelligence of natural laws and in thinking dialectically, I was convinced of the importance of using what was left after the destruction (the rich soil) and did not want to condemn nature for being cruel. Some of these accumulated experiences are discussed in detail in this appendix.

INTELLECTUAL IMPERIALISM

Being a graduate student in the Department of Measurement, Evaluation and Computer Applications (MECA) at OISE/UT (Ontario Institute for Studies in Education/University of Toronto) located me in the heart of the empire of figures and numbers, statistical designs and computer models and packages. I have always been impressed by Western efficiency, and I thought that by rooting my education in a "strong and solid" ground such as statistics and computer designs I might be able to improve and advance the methods of teaching and testing English as a second language in my country, Bahrain. I was convinced that statistical designs and "hard" data in testing and program evaluation might be the solution for some of the problems in education. Although I succeeded in passing the required courses in evaluation, I was dissatisfied with the academic situation. After analyzing the situation to find the source of my disenchantment, I realized that education was treated clearly in a very superficial and technical manner. Thus, the academic atmosphere as I experienced it was for me dry and intellectually unsatisfying.

Fortunately, academic life became more rewarding when I took some courses of a different approach outside MECA. Gradually, I discovered the strong relationship between people's research methods and their approach and attitude to education and to life in general. I started questioning the appropriateness of "scientific" research for the social sciences. The emphasis in most evaluation studies, even in the most reputable journals on evaluation and education, was on the accuracy of the design, efficiency, validity and reliability, and the statistical significance of the results. However, my mind was asking; "What about the meaning of the problem and its educational significance and usefulness to teachers for improving their programs?" As a teacher who is concerned about her students and about improving the teaching/learning relationship, I felt that the studies were not "real." Although some of the issues were relevant, the approaches for solving them were not practical. I felt frustrated, disheartened and disempowered; I lost confidence in myself as a student and a teacher. I wondered: "If I am so disempowered, how am I going to help my students?" I felt imprisoned intellectually. My mind was like a restless bird trying to break the bars of the imprisoning cage of scientific methods, a priori models and statistical analysis.

Out of desperation I tried to understand this intellectual crisis. For the first time I saw the similarity between political and intellectual imperialism. I began to wonder, to ask: "Why do we foreign students leave our countries and suffer so much for a piece of paper from Western universities? Why are we so dependent on the West, even intellectually?" When Al Azhar, the first Islamic University, was established in the 9th century CE, the West was mired in the dark ages. When the West woke up, it built its present scientific and technological civilization on Islamic knowledge that was transferred from Islam to Spain, then called Andalusia.

The answer is now a commonplace. The core of the problem, in my personal experience and the social experience of the Middle East, was "intellectual dependency." In an attempt to be "objective," I started to think and to analyze the situation according to Western standards. From a Western point of view, economic power and material development is what makes nations strong or dependent. The Middle East is one of the wealthiest regions of the world with all its natural resources. Why are Middle Eastern countries completely dependent on the West, even economically? From the Western point of view also, education is the key for individual development and empowerment. I was a doctoral candidate in one of the well-known universities in the West, so why was I feeling discouraged by and imprisoned in the knowledge to which I was exposed? If knowledge is power, why was I feeling helpless and disempowered?

Gradually, I began to distinguish between knowledge and information. I was receiving bits and pieces of information that were analyzed technically and measured superficially with statistical designs that researchers of the study themselves, both graduate students and even some professors, cannot analyze thoroughly without the extensive support of statistical experts and advisors. Knowledge is made to conform to technology and computer design. Because of the limitations of computer design, researchers are forced to simplify their questions and to ask only those that can be answered and handled by statistics. With the advancement of technology the situation has deteriorated and researchers have simplified their questions even more so as to be able to use computerized, statistical packages. The limitations of statistics were added to the limitations of computers. That was one of the reasons why I felt the absence of intellectuality in the Institute. Simple, straightforward questions do not need much intellectualizing. Despite the efficiency of computers and extremely impressive diagrams and tables they can produce, they are unable to encompass the complexity and wholeness of human problems and experiences. Computers and statistics were originally discovered to solve efficiently problems in the natural and physical sciences where phenomena to an extent are fixed and a cause and effect relationship can be established. Problems in social sciences are not as straight forward as those in the physical sciences.

What troubled me most about the academic situation was the paradox in the superficiality of knowledge and the prevailing arrogance that computerized pre-packaged designs create in researchers. A personal experience and a reflection on that experience made me aware of this phenomenon. Using SPSSX to analyze some data for an assignment in one of the measurement courses, I was impressed by the information and elegant tables and graphs that were produced by the package. In a moment of illusion and self-deceit I thought that I had generated the information, created the design and the graphs. Immediately after, I realized that I had just followed instructions and used a minimum of thinking to produce this impressive design which had my name attached to it to inflate the ego even more. The credit goes to the original designer of the package that I appreciate highly, but the rest of us, the "users" only follow instructions and use some thinking, to run computerized designs. Some of the thinking that is used is mainly to torture the data to fit the design. It is confining, rather than liberating thinking.

What troubled my soul even more was the lack of appreciation for intellectuality, genuine knowledge and use of the higher faculties of thinking by most package users. The domination and control of hard data and computerized packages are only a reflection of the predominant rule of economics and finance over cultural and liberal education in the outside world. Educators changed their direction to accommodate the financial, industrial world instead of trying to affect and change the outside world to be more humane and more real. The only reason for coming to the West and going through so much trouble is for intellectual development and empowerment through education. The paradoxical effect of disempowerment urged me to find an answer to such a confusing situation.

So, my feeling of disempowerment and disenchantment came from intellectual and psychological resistance to this kind of superficial knowledge. I could neither conform to that type of knowledge, nor confront such a "super power" of scientific imperialism that controlled the whole world. The result was an "intellectual crisis" and a rebellious researcher.

I started to ask: "What is democracy then? If it is not practiced in its birthplace, the universities, where is it going to be practiced, protected and developed? Where is freedom of speech? Where is intellectual freedom? Where is the right to treat all human beings equally. The leading question was: "Do I have to conform and do what everybody else is doing to be accepted in academic circles, or shall I set myself free?" And freedom was my choice.

SPRING 1988: KNOWLEDGE BASE EXPANSION

In one of my courses in the Spring of 1988, I was challenged to prove to a Western audience that Islam is not what is shown in the North American prejudiced media, that Islam has a great scientific and cultural civilization that went back fourteen hundred years. I also challenged myself to prove such a claim. I did not have any background in Islamic studies; my last contact with formal Arabic schooling ceased when I graduated from high school in Bahrain. Ever since, I had been either studying English, teaching English, or studying through the medium of English. When faced with this challenge, my first concern was the availability of references. Spending a few hours with the on-line catalog at the Robarts Library caused mixed feelings. The huge number of references, classic and contemporary, created both excitement and frustration. It was exciting to know about the availability of a wide range of references on Islamic studies in many areas and in different languages, English, Arabic and Persian among them. It was overwhelming because I realized the difficulty of the task I was undertaking and the seriousness of the challenge.

The task was difficult but successful, rewarding and stimulating. I was led to more research to understand Islamic theories and try to bring down Islamic philosophy from its ivory tower to meet educational practical needs. The result of this task was a term paper entitled "The Collapse of Westernized Universities in Islamic Societies: Part 1." The seed for the book in hand was planted then in that paper and nurtured by my professor, Dr. Ruth Hayhoe, whose teaching approach and diverse experiences in the East (China) and the West gave her a broad perspective on education and life. After reading my paper, she said, in a sympathetic voice: "Nothing will be the same again!" I did not, then, realize the depth of what she had said. She anticipated the difficulties for which I was heading and which I should be facing in the future. After the Spring of 1988 the direction and dimension of my research and my thinking changed. I consider that term paper a turning point in my life. It introduced me to many great Muslim philosophers about whom I had only heard and had never read or studied.

For the first time in many years I felt no barrier between my leisure time and study or work time. I spent long hours reading and quenching my everlasting thirst for knowledge from an Islamic fountain. I was like a wanderer in the desert who, after a long search for a sip of water, found an oasis in the middle of the desert. It was not a mirage this time. It was real. For the first time I felt united with myself after being split for so long. The mind and the soul were in perfect harmony. The enjoyment came not only from realizing the depth of those great minds, but also from reading the original texts in Arabic and enjoying the richness of the language and its ability to capture fully the essence of philosophical and intellectual concepts.

To give the reader an idea of my term paper I mentioned above, I quote here from the beginning:

> The purpose of this paper is (1) to examine the causes of decline of education in Muslim-Arab societies in the last two centuries; (2) to propose a multidimensional theory for education to cater to Islamic education. That is mainly because the existing limited education theories cannot reveal the multidimensionality of Islamic religion and consequently they do not encompass all aspects of Islamic education for Muslim students. Also, because imported theories are developed to cater to special needs in specific societies with specific educational philosophy as well as specific economic, social and political structure.[1]

The paper cited the causes of decline of education in Muslim-Arab countries in the 19th and 20th centuries as both external and internal. External factors are colonization and modernization. Internal factors are incongruity and lack of harmony between the original Islamic phi-

losophy of both the "perennial knowledge" and "acquired knowledge" as practiced within the Islamic framework, and the actual economic political, social and educational practice in Islamic countries.
The result has been the disempowerment of countries that, despite
their natural resources, are dependent economically, intellectually and
even psychologically on their former colonizers to supply them with
food, ideas, books, educational design, teachers and confidence, as
well. The West became the standard against which everything is measured. Anything approved by the West means a high standard.
Graduates from Western universities are highly regarded, whereas
graduates from Arab universities or other Islamic countries are
regarded as second-class citizens in academic circles and in society.
Such control from the ex-colonizers could not have been permitted
and maintained if it had not been supported and encouraged by local
authorities. I experienced disempowerment both at the political level
in the Middle East and at the academic, intellectual level in the West,
all of which caused the eruption of the volcano.

SUMMER 1988: THE PARADIGM SHIFT

During the Summer of 1988 there was great pressure on the volcano
inside me. I was boiling with new ideas and old feelings. The interaction between political imperialism and intellectual imperialism was
intense. In the midst of confusion and struggle, as I was trying to
choose an evaluation method that suited my thesis topic, I was also
trying to write a tentative proposal and to form a thesis committee,
suddenly several doors were opened, and I was swept into a new era of
research and methods of inquiry; an era that dealt with an alternative
paradigm for human and social sciences. Three major events highlight
this new era of my intellectual journey which shone like a bright star in
the sky of my life, a star that was hidden behind heavy clouds of intellectual and political imperialism. This period was the immediate cause
for the eruption of the volcano.

   During this period of intense intellectual, spiritual and psychological experiences, I felt that the gateway to knowledge was opened to me
suddenly. After reflection, I can distinguish three landmarks that
influenced my thinking and my research, and have continued to enrich

my research and my intellectual journey ever since. These events were the discovery of 1) alternative paradigm and interpretive/naturalistic research methods; 2) personal practical knowledge and narrative inquiry as research methods; 3) social knowledge and the Frankfurt School.

ALTERNATIVE PARADIGM: THE TURNING POINT

This new era in research methods for me started with discovering Guba and Lincoln's books on naturalistic evaluation, *Effective Evaluation*[2] and *Naturalistic Inquiry*[3]. What makes these two books unique in qualitative research methods is the intellectual and philosophical base of the inquiry. The emphasis is on paradigm rather than method. They propose an alternative paradigm which allows for deeper and more meaningful questions in the social sciences and the empowerment of both the researcher and the participants. The references of the two books flooded me with a wide range of relevant literature. Immediately afterwards, my supervisor introduced me to Helen Simons' book on democratic evaluation: *Getting to Knowing Schools in a Democracy*[4]. This important book encourages democracy and empowerment of teachers as evaluators of their own programs, which was the particular aim of my search.

AVENUES TO PERSONAL AND SOCIAL KNOWLEDGE

The second important event was to be introduced to Personal Practical Knowledge (PPK) by my professor, Dr. Michael Connelly. Personal Practical Knowledge was an area that opened new avenues in my research and gave a new direction to research methods in education. The power of personal practical knowledge lies in how the concept of totality captures the past, the present and the future by reconstructing the past in the light of the present to form an insightful future by understanding and planning. The concept of totality appropriately fitted in the holistic framework of the study. I embraced some of these ideas wholeheartedly because they mirrored my ideas of 'wholeness,' 'democracy,' 'humanity' and 'morality' in education. I felt empowered because I was able to articulate my personal ideas confidently without being accused of being 'emotional,' 'personal' and 'passionate' in the 'scientific' world of hard data and objectivity.

The third major event in the new era of research methods was my attending a course on language, power and learning by a visiting professor from Australia in the Summer of 1988. Dr. Robert Connell introduced me to another sea of knowledge, an area that blends language and power strongly and reveals through the literature the power of analyzing knowledge production and the delivery of knowledge by specific use of language. The focus of the course was on the linguistic turn in social theory, theories of discourse, language and democracy, language in the sociology of education and language and social practices.

This course introduced me to *The Archeology of Knowledge* by Michael Foucault; *Knowledge and Control* by M. Young; *Ways with Words* by Shirley Heath; *Restructuring of Social and Political Theory* by R. Bernstein; *Communication and Evolution of Society*; and *The Theory of Communicative Action* by Jürgen Habermas. In this course I realized that the roots of a communicative approach to language teaching (that I had adopted in 1981 in my MA thesis) lay at the heart of social theories.

THE QUEST FOR TRUTH, UNITY AND HARMONY

The previous section traced the immediate roots of the intellectual development of the study. The following section reveals older and more permanent roots that developed the ideas of wholeness and multidimensionality, dialectical and hermeneutics. Although chronologically the previous section of my intellectual journey comes later than this section, the realization of the roots of the ideas presented here came later in the journey of development. So to give a 'faithful presentation' of human development, confusion and the element of uncertainty that prevails in our thinking, the portrait of self-realization is described as it occurred. Experiences and their roots are intermingled in a complicated way such that any strict categorization of time or space tends to create a distorted image and invalid interpretation. Therefore, the following section describes the journey of development in the ideas of wholeness, multidimensionality and dialectical thinking.

Totality, wholeness, integrity, unity, connectedness, harmony, continuity and interaction are all key words in this book. However, wholeness and integration of knowledge, are the main issues. In tracing the roots of these issues, I realized that my education in the East and the West caused a split in my consciousness. The ideas of wholeness were not very clear from the beginning, and they evolved into different shapes and at different levels. Gradually, as the experiences unfold, what was lying deep in my subconscious was revealed and the idea of wholeness took its present shape.

To chart the journey of this intellectual development, I quote extracts from two letters I sent to the members of my thesis committee. One is the covering letter for the thesis proposal dated August 25th, 1988. The second is the covering letter for the report after Phase 1 of data collection, dated February 13, 1989. Both letters express the idea of wholeness, at different levels. I start with the first letter to the committee members.

> My educational experience enjoyed the best of the two worlds, the East and the West. At the same time it suffered and was torn between the East and the West. Since I was 17, I have been wandering the world, between the Middle East, Europe, and North America, trying to understand myself and the world around me. Going back and forth from one extreme to another, two conflicting extremes: Different value systems, different lifestyles, different languages, different mentalities, different weather too.
>
> During my journey, I suffered severely, not so much from culture shock, but mainly from intellectual and spiritual shocks. When I am in the West I could not understand why people cannot see things differently, and when I am in the East, I could not understand why people do not do things differently. I was never sure what 'differently' meant to me then. I had this strange feeling that Westerners feel with their minds and Easterners think with their hearts. Something was missing but I could not figure it out then.
>
> At last, after many years of formal schooling and work experience I came to realize that the 'whole' is missing. Reconciliation between the mind and the soul should take place in order to have the whole. As human beings we have both in our body. We have mind and we have soul. We understand certain things through our mind which can be

analyzed logically and transferred to language and number or what Polanyi calls 'propositional knowledge,' and I call 'intellectual knowledge.' On the other hand, there are certain things that cannot be understood and analyzed through logic or language. Things that we feel but cannot express. These I call 'spiritual knowledge' and Polanyi calls 'tacit knowledge.' The essence of my proposal is this 'whole mind' approach which can be achieved through a naturalistic, holistic, analytical, responsive approach.[5]

In this first letter I tried to highlight the conflict between the two extremes, the East and the West, and why my thesis proposal was about "reconciliation between the mind and the soul that should take place in order to have the whole." The journey for reconciliation starts from inside out. My realization of the importance of integration on the personal level was the first step in a long journey of self-discovery and self-development, of becoming whole instead of being fragmented and torn between the different levels of experiences—intellectual, spiritual and physical. To study any situation holistically we, as researchers in the social sciences, have to be aware of ourselves as whole human beings; otherwise we will not be able to grasp the essence and the depth of our existence and our experiences.

For it is essential that we should develop an art of education which will lead us out of the social chaos into which we have fallen during the last few years and decades. And the only way out of this social chaos is to bring spirituality into the souls of men through education, so that out of the spirit itself men may find the way to progress and to further evolution of civilization.[6]

Personal development goes hand in hand with social development. Realizing the importance of the wholeness of human beings led gradually to realizing the importance of the wholeness and integration of the education system in any society. This connection came after my preliminary analysis of the data collected in Phase 1. In the covering letter of the report to the committee members on February 13th, 1989, I addressed this issue:

The dilemma of Islamic societies lies partly in the fact that they imported secular education systems and planted them in the heart of Islamic traditional societies. To me it is like planting a palm tree in Alaska and expecting it to grow naturally and to give fruit as well. The mismatch between the religious foundation of Islamic societies and the secular building of the Western education system is a major cause of the problems encountered by our universities. The lack of harmony between people's lives outside the university and inside it, and the conflict between the two extremes, the secular and the religious, confuses everybody. Integrating spirituality into education was a new light for me in my experiences in the West, a new hope to achieve 'wholeness' in this fragmented world. I experienced the pain of unfulfillment spiritually and intellectually both in the East and the West. The materialistic overtone of the West pushed spirituality out of the curricula, so that any interest in the spiritual was to be an extra curricula activity. On the other hand, denial of freedom of speech in the East was a barrier to intellectual development and growth. Every issue is categorized as 'forbidden' or 'taboo,' politically, socially or religiously, according to interpretations of religious or political authorities.7

Going back and forth between the two extremes caused me torment and an inner feeling of being split in two. That caused confusion and disturbance at certain stages of my life. But from pain new branches always grow. That confusion and pain urged me to search for the causes, to understand the source of the pain and the reason for the struggle.

ANSWERING CRUCIAL QUESTIONS

In my search for truth, harmony and unity, I realized that the conflict and struggle came from a deep-rooted resistance to control of freedom. In the West, I felt my spiritual development and freedom in danger. In the East I felt my intellectual development and freedom to be in jeopardy. Did I have to give up one for the sake of keeping and developing the other? The fear of either/or was there; but struggle and resistance were there too, fighting against the split. I was faced with crucial questions: "Do I have to give up my Islamic Arabic, Eastern identity for the sake of getting higher education? Do I have to sacrifice my intellectual development and my thirst for knowledge for the sake of keeping my identity?"

The answer came in the form of a third question: "Why not keep both?" To answer this question was not easy, but the fact that the same questions were emerging at the social level in this study helped me to understand the situation better and try to find realistic solutions for the dilemma: how to preserve traditional cultures, while at the same time develop a new, 'modern' society. The question at the social level was: "Do we, as a non-Western society have to give up our language, culture and religion for the sake of economic development that comes from the West through the English language and a Western, secular educational system?"

There was a great struggle and conflict before each stage of harmony and unity, but eventually peace, as it should, came naturally through communication, interaction, reflection and understanding. So reflection on my personal experiences opened my mind and heart to an analysis of the socio-cultural situation in Bahrain and how that was affected by my personal experiences. A breakthrough came when I started to see myself as a microcosm and Bahrain as a macrocosm. I was torn between preserving my Islamic identity while looking for self-development at different levels. Bahrain also wished to keep its traditional, religious society, while striving for development at the same time.

For many reasons, keeping and preserving a cultural, traditional, religious society was associated with the East, whereas change and development, both secular and modern were associated with the West. So the conflict was between the Islamic religious society and the Western secular educational system. The pull and push was intensified between industrial developed countries and traditional, developing countries. Looking at the whole picture explains the appropriateness of personal experiences to the socio-cultural experiences of Bahrain. A quotation from Schutz shows the universality of such an idea.

> I simply take it for granted that other men also exist in this my world, and indeed not only in a bodily manner like and among other objects, but rather as endowed with a consciousness that is essentially the same as mine. Thus from the outset, my life-world is not my private world

but, rather, is intersubjective, the fundamental structure of its reality is that it is shared by us.[8]

KEEPING THE BALANCE

During Phase 11 of data collection, the hermeneutic nature of a naturalistic approach and the ongoing reflection on the data, caused me to realize that it is not only the West that has a mistaken idea of the concept of Islamic education. The majority of Muslim participants with whom I discussed the issue had the same misconception, that Islamic education means religious education. That meant reevaluating the idea of Islamic education at this stage of the study. What helped to keep a balance in the research is the wide-range selection of participants, whose points of view varied from the very philosophical to the very practical.

My responsibility was to keep the balance. Some participants explained how Arabization, as related directly to Islamic education, was not possible under present conditions, and we, Arabs, had to follow the West if we wanted to develop. The party opposed to Westernization drifted to the other extreme, and suggested that the only way for development was by Arabizing the university and society. They demanded revival of Arabic language and Islamic culture as the first step in this direction. The first aim in reconciliation was to keep the balance between scientific education and religious education, intellectuality and spirituality. However, I had to face the fact that the present situation at the University of Bahrain is off balance. Spirituality does not have any place in the curriculum except in the Islamic Education Department. In addition, the main issue was not *whether* to include Islamic studies or not, but the method of teaching the subject and its eventual aim.

Reconciliation is not easy for anybody. However, it should not be confused with compromise. To compromise connotes giving up something willingly or unwillingly for the sake of getting something else. The idea of giving up something creates deep silent aggression that can rise and explode at any time. Reconciliation however, means reaching to a deeper level of *understanding*, an understanding that analyzes personal opinions and prejudice in the light of universal knowledge. If there is any trace of compromise in this situation, it is the abandoning of prejudices and closed-mindedness for the sake of realizing the truth. At the beginning, there was a war between conflicting ideas. The first step in reconciliation came when I had to write a paper for the Seventh World Congress of Comparative Education, on June 26, 1989, in Montreal. I was convinced that by applying the methodological principles of hermeneutics, my understanding of the situation could increase. Deep down I felt at ease. For the first time after many years I was content with the resolution, as the following suggest.

> Therefore, the goal of locating this study in hermeneutics is to increase my understanding of how the East and the West come to misconstrue and misunderstand each other. Hermeneutics in this study is concerned with interpretation of human experience and the struggle to understand the conflicts between the East and the West. Being the child of the East and the West, I had learned to compare languages, cultures, histories, mentalities, personalities and schools of thoughts. In an attempt to understand the controversies of the two extremes, the East and the West, my two 'selves' were in continuous dialogue, even conflict.
>
> Since the method in hermeneutics is dialogue, and questions are answered through the dialectic of exchange between two subjects, what I am presenting here is the interpretation of this dialectic. After many years of being torn between the two worlds of extremes—the religious, spiritual East and the secular, material oriented West—I decided to reconcile the two instead of struggling against them. I realized that the dialectic between my two selves should be a dialectic of love and not of hate. The struggle should be 'for' the ideal and not 'against' it, whether in the East or the West. I realized that my longtime struggle was rooted in feelings of insecurity that I might lose my Islamic/Arabic eastern identity in the West.9

Steele affirms:

> Hermeneutics has expanded beyond its origins in textual interpretation and become a discipline concerned with interpretation of human products and experiences. There would be no need of hermeneutics if we did not ask questions about ourselves, but we do.... Modern hermeneutics provides methodological guidelines for asking and

answering questions.... The method is dialogue. Questions are answered through the give and take discussion, through the dialectics of exchange between two subjects.... We learn nothing, if we do not question. If we do not let others or ourselves question us, then we remain forever unchanged. To let the other speak and try our best to hear is the difficult task that hermeneutics sets for us.... The goal of hermeneutics is to increase human understanding by questioning how we come to misconstrue, disagree, agree, understand and reach consensus.[10]

To embrace the conception of dialectics wholeheartedly at this stage was the natural thing to do. My experiences in the East and the West had gradually developed my dialectic thinking, without being aware of the process. Living as I do in two different and contradictory situations has created polarity in thinking. Polarity causes pull and push, conflict, struggle and war inside a person. Being driven to one pole away from the other, however, might not create a crisis or conflict because the decision might be made to belong to one camp or another without much struggle. So, the conflict starts when a person experiences the advantages and disadvantages of the two contradicting situations. When the choice is between two parts of one's being, the soul and the mind, the spiritual and intellectual, the crisis is great.

CREATING THE FRAMEWORK

To be so confused and torn between the mind and the soul is not a comfortable state of mind. It was only after reading Michael Basseches' book *Dialectical Thinking and Adult Development,* in October 1989 that I was able to create the framework for my personal experiences and for my thesis. Only then was I able to articulate my ideas and to conceptualize them. Discovering Basseches' book was like finding a secure home for my dispersed ideas, torn between two extremes at many levels: personal, social and universal. I realized that dialectical thinking was the last stage in adult development and that I was going through a natural process of that development. It was a relief to know that the pain, the conflict, the struggle, the confusion, the contradictions and the pull of the extremes were only stages that dialectical thinkers experience. I desperately needed assurance that the crisis that I was undergoing was not a negative one. That assurance came from Riegel who expressed a similar idea:

> But such conflicts and crises are not to be regarded in a negative manner. Most crises represent constructive confrontations in which the discordance and contradiction generated provide the source of every new change both within the individual and within society. Thereby, the interactions of conflicting events are transformed into coordinated patterns of relationships and meanings. These synchronizing leaps of development represent the most important achievements of the individual and society.[11]

Reflecting on the stages of intellectual development of my work shows that the seeds for dialectical thinking were there from the beginning. The seeds had to go through the natural processes of incubation and germination. The concept of 'wholeness' itself is dialectical. My thesis proposal for a 'whole mind' approach, in August 1988, and my attempt at reconciliation between the mind and soul, was dialectics in action. My appeal to the committee members, in February 1989, to work together toward a mutual understanding of the East and the West was dialectic thinking.

MY BILINGUAL HOME: THE BIRTH OF DIALECTICAL THINKING

Three major factors contributed to the development of my dialectical thinking: a bilingual and bicultural upbringing, diverse educational experiences, in the East and the West, and the interpretive methods of inquiry and reflection on personal experience.

The birthplace for dialectical thinking was the bilingual and bicultural home in which I was brought up, with two languages and cultures—Arabic and Persian—and Islam as the common factor. Having a bilingual mother and a multilingual father whose extensive travels frequently included the children, significantly broadened my horizon and opened my eyes to a variety of cultures, languages, lifestyles and ideas. Accepting differences was second nature to me. The dialectics then was of love and understanding.

As a child I accepted my colorful experiences because none of them was a threat. Children are quick learners; they are good listeners and observers too. They are receptive, joyful, humorous and flexible. It is our rigid education system that makes us narrow-minded, and prey to prejudice and resentment. By imposing rigid rules, such a system chains the creative minds of children and captures their free souls. The home where I was brought up, freed my mind and my soul for exploration.

I can now see that both my parents were dialectical practitioners. Despite being conservative and maintaining rules and regulations for our lives, they were open-minded in accepting innovations in lifestyles and ideas as long as they did not contradict our belief system. They rooted me firmly in my religion and in both languages, and then left me free to grow and flourish according to my abilities. My parents were aware of the importance of preserving and developing one's culture, language and religion. At the same time, they realized the natural desire for development and the need for changes in any human being and society. They not only gave me the freedom to grow, but supported me all the way through. They kept the balance between the firmness of our roots and the flexibility needed for growing new branches. The seeds of dialectical thinking were planted and nourished by the warmth of their hearts and love.

Second, my diverse education in the Middle East, Europe and North America was a second major factor in developing dialectical thinking. Living in different parts of the world, and experiencing a variety of languages, cultures and ways of thinking provided intellectual enrichment. The diverse and even conflicting educational systems to which I was exposed contributed to the process of dialectics. The torment, the pain and the struggle in contradictory environments forced me to seek solutions. Reflection on the historical process of my personal experience helped in crystallizing my dialectical thinking. As Basseches states:

> From the perspective of dialectical thinking, what it is that remains recognizable across a range of changes is the historical process as an evolving whole. Any changes at all, no matter how radical, can be equilibrated if it can be conceptualized as a moment in a dialectical process of evolution. New events are integrated within dialectical conception of a process as later steps in the evolution of that process; old

constructions are conserved-they remain part of the process of dialectic-although their historical role is reconstructed in the light of subsequent transformations.[12]

Finally, the naturalistic method of inquiry and reflection on personal experience is the third major factor in my dialectical development. Dialogue is a hermeneutic method, where questions are answered through the dialectic of exchanges, as Steele suggests.[13] Hermeneutics is embedded in naturalistic inquiry. Communication and dialogue are important aspects in this methodology that helped me in building strong relationships with the participants in my study so that they could discuss issues freely without the restrictions of pre-designed models and questionnaires.

Listening to a wide range of opinions caused a lot of confusion at the outset, although it was only a stage in the development of dialectical thinking. Such conflicting ideas and opinions among the participants indicate the diversity in any society regarding controversial issues. The urge to know the "reality" leads us as inquirers to be dialectical because the truth for students is not the same as for administrators, teachers or even parents. Research cannot survive such diversity of opinion unless researchers learn to work through the dialectical, accept contradictions and realize that all participants have the right to tell their side of the story. If dialogue is a characteristic of naturalistic inquiry, monologue is a characteristic of reflection on personal experiences. The continuous silent hermeneutics that takes place inwardly creates a deeper understanding of the conflict between opposing ideas. The genuine quest for the truth eventually leads to the middle road where extremes are reconciled. It leads to the "straight path" according to Islam.

MULTIDIMENSIONALITY AND WHOLENESS

From an analysis of my experiences, I discovered that I had had an obsession with the idea of multidimensionality that developed gradually to an "intellectual passion," to use Polanyi's term: a passion that urged me to search for wholeness in everything. It was this intellectual passion for wholeness that was responsible, partly, for the intellectual crisis. I discovered that the pain of unfulfilment, intellectually and spiritually, was caused by the predominant unidimensional approaches to education, measurement and evaluation. I was torn between being aware of the multidimensionality of life and educational issues in reality, and witnessing the unidimensional approaches used and advocated by the majority of those in academia. I investigated this issue at different levels and different areas in some of the term papers that I submitted as course requirements during the academic year 1985-86. The following is an extract from one paper that discusses the issue of multidimensionality and curriculum evaluation as a means for course development:

> Multidimensionality is, in fact, an important characteristic of teaching-learning procedure in general, and of curriculum evaluation in particular. When teachers think of the success of their courses, the first thing that comes to their mind is to measure the students' mastery of certain items included in the syllabus. Testing the students mastery level, of course, is only one of several dimensions of curriculum evaluation. Therefore, by testing students' performance we are addressing only one dimension of program evaluation's multidimensional feature.
>
> Obviously, by applying a unidimensional instrument to measure a multidimensional-featured discipline, we will not be able to look at the problem from different angles; to have a clear and well-rounded picture. Consequently our judgment and decision for improving that program will not be effective.[14]

THE UNIVERSALITY OF PERSONAL KNOWLEDGE

Reflection on personal experiences can be as confining as any other mode of inquiry if it does not extend to the outside world and relate to the society to which one belongs. It can, in fact, lead gradually in the direction of narcissistic preoccupation with subjective feelings and experience. Events in the community, the society, even the world, are the criteria and the test for the importance of our personal experiences and concerns. Conferences are recognizable events in the academic field, where scholars gather to present their latest findings and discuss their ideas based on personal, academic or social concerns. Conferences are also a place for debating controversial issues. Careful and diverse selection of the sessions and seminars that include topics in which we, as participants, are not interested as well as topics in which we are interested, can prove valuable and eye-opening, because it gives us the chance to listen to the opinions of the "other side" of the issues.

During 1989, I attended six different conferences in North America, the Middle East and Europe. The conferences related directly or indirectly to education and to issues associated with the alternative paradigm, fragmentation of knowledge and comparative education. I should like to share with the reader the reaction of some the participants to issues of Islamic development. The conference that I attended in the Summer of 1989 was in Montreal: The VIIth World Congress of Comparative Education Development, Communication and Language, June 26-30, 1989. University of Montreal, Canada. I presented my paper on 'The Collapse of Westernized Universities in Islamic Society: Part 2.' Because of controversial issues presented in that paper, I had strong reactions from two westerners. One was a woman who taught for some time in educational institutions in Kuwait and believed strongly that the East could not survive or develop without Western education. She was aggressive and presented her views very emotionally and unacademically. She insisted, however, that universities in the West had been built originally on religious foundations. Another audience participant from the United States, who taught at the American University in Cairo (AUC), believed that I was doing the Arab nation a disservice if I advocated a return to Arabic language and Islamic education, because it prevented economic development in the region. Both participants were live examples of the reaction my thesis would be facing in the East and the West. They were typical of the Western "experts" that are hired by almost all developing countries to develop their education systems. They have the illusion of knowing best how to run other peoples' lives, without even attempting to communicate with them or understanding the opinion of the people on whom they impose their models.

To sum up, reflection on past experiences revealed the intermingled relationship between my personal experience and Bahrain's social experience. The wealth of experiences and knowledge that I gained during the Summer of 1988 and the pressure that such a load put on past experiences caused the eruption of the volcano and marked a new era in the history of my life. My intellectual and spiritual crisis forced me to reflect and think of the causes. Intellectual and scientific imperialism was the major reason, and it was directly related to political imperialism in the Middle East and other oppressed countries. So the problem was personal and social. The questions of this study emerged from the intersection of the personal concerns of the researcher and the social concerns of Bahraini society. The feeling of disempowerment and imprisonment forced me to look for an answer. The answers poured down like spring showers. Within three months I regained my lost confidence and control over the study that I wanted to do. I was able to ask my questions and not be forced to dilute, simplify and fragment them to meet the requirements of computerized statistical packages. Freedom from intellectual imperialism was the empowerment for which I was striving, and that freedom I gained. As Aime` Ce`saire said: "There are two ways of losing oneself: Through fragmentation in the particular or dilution in the universal."[15]

NOTES

AUTHOR'S INTRODUCTION

1   Guba, Egon G. and Lincoln, Yvonna S., *Naturalistic Inquiry* (Beverley Hills, CA: Sage Publications, 1985).

CHAPTER ONE

1   Al Zeera, Z., 'Evaluation of the Orientation Program at the University of Bahrain: A Socio-Cultural Perspective,' (PhD Thesis, University of Toronto, Canada: 1990).

2   Polanyi, Michael, *Personal Knowledge: Towards a Post-Critical Philosophy* (Chicago, IL: University of Chicago Press, 1958), p.3.

3   Morgan, Gareth, (ed.), *Beyond Method: Strategies for Social Research* (Beverley Hills, CA: Sage Publications, 1983), p.398.

4   Pellegrini, A.D., *Narrative Thought and Narrative Language*, eds. Bruce Britton & A.D. Pellegrini (Hillsdale, NJ: Lawrence Erlbam Associates, 1990), p.222.

CHAPTER TWO

1   Nasr, Seyyed Hossein (ed.), *Islamic Spirituality: Foundations*, vol. 19 of *World Spirituality: An Encyclopedic History of the Religious Quest* (New York: Crossroad, 1987), p.xxi.

2   This is an extract from correspondence between the author and Dr. Dolores Furlong, Assistant Dean of the Renaissance College, University of New Brunswick, in April 1998.

3   Sherif, Mohamed Ahmed, *Ghazali's Theory of Virtue* (Albany, NY: State University of New York Press, 1975), p.157.

4   Ibid.

5   Maspero, H., *Taoism and Chinese Religion* (Amerhurst: University of Massachusetts Press, 1981), p.73.

CHAPTER THREE

1   Guba, E., *The Paradigm Dialog* (Newbury Park, CA: Sage Publications, 1990).

2   Guba, E. and Lincoln, Yvonna, S., *Effective Evaluation* (San Francisco, CA: Jossey-Bass Publishers, 1981), p.28.

3   Ibid.

4   Tesch, Renata, *Qualitative Research: Analysis Types and Software Tools* (New York: Falmer Press, 1990).

5   Simons, Helen, *Getting to Know*

Schools in a Democracy: The Politics and Process of Evaluation (New York: Falmer Press, 1987).

6 MacDonald, B., 'Briefing Decision Makers,' in *School Evaluation: The Politics and Process*, ed. E.R. House (Berkeley, CA: McCutchan, 1973). See also by the same author, 'Evaluation and Control of Education,' in *SAFARI 1: Innovation, Evaluation, Research and the Problem of Control* (Norwich: Center for Applied Research in Education, University of East Anglia, 1974); 'The Experience of Innovation,' in *CARE Occasional Publications No. 6* (Norwich: Center for Applied Research in Education, University of East Anglia, 1978).

7 Parlett, M. and Hamilton, D., 'Evaluation as Illumination,' in *Ocassional Paper 9* (Center for Research in the Educational Sciences, University of Edinburgh, 1972).

8 Stake, R., *Evaluating the Arts in Education* (Colombus, OH: Charles E. Merrill Publishing Company, 1975).

9 Kelly, E.F., 'Curriculum Evaluation and Literary Criticism,' in *Curriculum Theory Network 5* (1975).

10 Rippey, R. (ed.), *Studies in Transactional Evaluation* (Berkeley, CA: McCutchan, 1973).

11 Eisner, E., 'Educational Connoisseurship and Criticism,' in *Qualitative Approaches to Evaluation*, ed. David Fetterman (New York: Praeger, 1976).

12 Wolf, R., 'The Use of Judicial Evaluation Methods in the Formation of Education Policy,' in *Educational Evaluation and Policy Analysis*, 1 (May–June, 1974).

13 See Guba & Lincoln, *Effective Evaluation*; and Guba and Lincoln, *Naturalistic Inquiry*.

14 See Tesch, *Qualitative Research*.

15 Guba & Lincoln, *Naturalistic Inquiry*, p.28.

16 Deutscher, I., 'Words and Deeds: Social Science and Social Policy,' in *Qualitative Methodology*, ed. W. Filstead (Chicago, IL: Markham, 1970).

17 Ibid. p.33.

18 Guba, *The Paradigm Dialog*, p.27.

19 Guba & Lincoln, *Effective Evaluation*.

20 See Eisner, Elliot W. & Peshkin, Alan (eds.), *Qualitative Inquiry in Education: The Continuing Debate* (New York: Teachers' College, Columbia University, 1990); and Guba, *The Paradigm Dialog*.

21 Patton, Michael Quinn, *Qualitative Evaluation Methods* (Beverley Hills, CA: Sage Publications, 1980), p.28.

22 Polanyi, Michael, *Beyond Nihilism* (Cambridge: University Press, 1960).

23 Hjartland, L., 'Statistics as Fragmentors of Knowledge,' paper

presented at a meeting of the *International Conference for Social Philosophy on Fragmentation of Knowledge*, Capri, Italy, June 18–23, 1989, p.3.

24 Ibid, p.4.

25 Cited in Raskin, Marcus G. and others, *New Ways of Knowing: The Sciences, Society and Reconstructive Knowledge* (Totowa, NJ: Rowman & Littlefield, 1987), pp.247–248.

26 Ibid, p.249.

27 Eisner, E. *The Educational Imagination* (New York: Macmillan Publishing Company, 1985), p.20.

28 Raskin, *New Ways of Knowing*, p.160.

29 Eisner, *The Educational Imagination*, p.218.

30 Raskin, *New Ways of Knowing*, p.26.

31 King, K., 'Two Key Fragmentations: That Between Experimental Science and Social Science and that Between Western and Third World Science,' paper presented at a meeting of the *International Institute for Social Philosophy on Fragmentation of Knowledge*, Capri, Italy, June 18–23, 1989, p.3.

32 Apple, M., *Ideology and Curriculum* (New York: Routledge, 1990).

33 Scriven, M., 'Objectivity and Subjectivity in Social Research,' in *Philosophical Redirection of Social Research*, ed. L.G. Thomas (Chicago: University of Chicago Press, 1972), p.27.

34 See Guba & Lincoln, *Effective Evaluation*, (1981).

35 Patton, *Qualitative Evaluation Methods*, (1980).

36 Important and thorough sources for such information are M. Lecompt, *Handbook of Qualitative Research in Education* (1992); J. Kirk, *Reliability and Validity in Qualitative Research* (1986); B. Berg, *Qualitative Research Methods for the Social Sciences* (1989); I. Holloway, *Basic Concepts for Qualitative Research* (1997); and N. Denzin, *The Handbook of Qualitative Research* (1994).

37 Guba & Lincoln, *Effective Evaluation*.

38 Ibid.

39 Ibid, p.86.

40 Ibid, p.88.

41 Ibid, p.87.

42 Bronfenbrenner, V., 'Toward an Experimental Ecology of Human Development,' *American Psychologist*, vol.32, no.7 (1977), p.513.

43 Lincoln, Y. & Guba, E., 'But is it Rigorous? Trustworthiness and Authenticity in Naturalistic Evaluation,' *New Directions for Program Evaluation*, no.30 (June 1986), p.76.

44 Ibid, p.79.

45 Ibid, p.82.

CHAPTER FOUR

1   Lincoln & Guba, 'But is it Rigorous?,' p.65.
2   Nasr, Seyyed Hossein, *Knowledge and the Sacred* (Albany, NY: State University of New York Press, 1989), p.133.
3   Guba, *The Paradigm Dialog*, p.20.
4   Nasr, Seyyed Hossein, *Islamic Science, An Illustrated Study* (London: World of Islam Festival Publication Company, 1976), p.3.
5   Banaie, M. and Haque, N., *From Facts to Values: Certainty, Order, Balance and their Universal Implications* (Toronto, Canada: Optagon Publications, 1995).
6   Ibid, p.122.
7   Ibid, p.44.
8   Readers interested in this topic can refer to a large number of books written recently on the damage that Western scientific thinking has done to humanity; for example: J. Saul, *Voltaire's Bastards*; H. Marcuse, *One Dimensional Man*; J. Habermas, *Communicative Competence*.

CHAPTER FIVE

1   Nasr, *Islamic Spirituality*, p.xv.
2   al-Fārūqī, Ismaʿīl R. & Lois Lamyāʾ, *The Cultural Atlas of Islam*, (New York: Macmillan, 1986), p.iv.
3   Mutahhari, M., *Foundations of Islamic Thought* (Berkeley, CA: Mizan Press, 1985), p. 54.
4   Habermas, Jürgen, *The Theory of Communicative Action*. Trans-lated by Thomas McCarthy (Boston, MA: Beacon Press, 1984), p.205.
5   Ibid, pp 205-211.
6   Ibid.
7   al-Fārūqī, *The Cultural Atlas of Islam*, p.79.
8   Mahdi, M., 'The New Wisdom: Synthesis of Philosophy and Mysticism,' *The Encyclopaedia Britannica*, vol. 22 (1987), p.27.
9   al-Fārūqī, Ismaʿīl R. and Nasseef, Abdullah Omar, (eds.), *Social and Natural Sciences: The Islamic Perspective* (Jeddah: Hodder & Stoughton, King Abdulaziz University, 1981), p.17. Emphasis added.
10   Sharif, M.M. (ed.), *A History of Muslim Philosophy: With Short Accounts of Other Disciplines and the Modern Renaissance in Muslim Lands* (Wiesbaden: Harrassowitz, 1963).
11   Ibid, p.11. Emphasis added.
12   Ibid.
13   Umaruddin, M., *The Ethical Philosophy of al-Ghazzali* (Aligarh, India: Muslim University, 1962), p.64.
14   Naqvi, Syed Nawab Haider, *Ethics and Economics: An Islamic Synthesis* (Leicester, UK: Islamic Foundation, 1981), p.152.
15   Daoudi, Mahmoud, 'An Intro-duction to the Implications of Human Nature for Ibn Khaldun's Thinking,' *The Islamic Quarterly*, vol.32, no.1 (1988), p.15.
16   Ibid, p. 10.

17 Murata, S., 'Masculine-Feminine
     Complementary in the Spiritual
     Psychology of Islam,' *The Islamic
     Quarterly*, vol.33, no.3 (1989),
     p.171.
18 Ibid, p.175.

CHAPTER SIX

1   Eaton, C.G., 'Man' in *Islamic
     Spirituality: Foundations*, ed.
     Seyyed Hossein Nasr, p.358.
2   Nasr, Seyyed Hossein, *Islamic
     Spirituality: Foundations*, p.xviii.
3   Langgulung, Hassan, 'Ibn Sina as
     an Educationist,' *The Islamic
     Quarterly*, vol. 32, no. 2 (1988).
4   Nasr, *Islamic Spirituality*, p.345.
5   Abdul Haleem, M., 'The Hereafter
     and the Here-and-Now in the
     Qur'an,' *The Islamic Quarterly*,
     vol. 33, no. 2 (1989), p. 119.
6   Murata, 'Masculine-Feminine
     Complementary,' p. 182.
7   Nasr, *Islamic Spirituality*, p.xv.
8   For further details, see Sherif,
     Ghazali's Theory of Virtue.

CHAPTER SEVEN

1   Tibawi, A. L., *Islamic Education:
     Its Traditions and Modernization
     into the Arab National Systems*
     (London: Luzac, 1972), p.40.
2   Mutahhari, *Foundations of
     Islamic Thought*, p. 61.
3   Sharif, *A History of Muslim
     Philosophy*, p.495.
4   Ibid, p.496.
5   Al-Ghazālī, M., *Mizān al-ʿAmal*
     (Cairo: Dar al-Ma'arif, 1964),

p.35.
6   Umaruddin, M., *The Ethical
     Philosophy of al-Ghazzali*.
7   Mutahhari, *Foundations of
     Islamic Thought*, p.25.
8   Sharif, *History of Muslim
     Philosophy*.
9   Nasr, *Knowledge and the Sacred*,
     p. 48.
10 Sardar, Ziauddin, (ed.), *The
     Revenge of Athena: Science,
     Exploitation, and the Third World*
     (London: Mansell Publishing Ltd.,
     1988).
11 See Nasr, *Islamic Science*; also
     *An Introduction to Islamic
     Cosmological Doctrines:
     Conceptions of Nature and
     Methods Used for its Study by the
     Ikhwan al-Safa,' al-Bīrūnī, and
     Ibn Sina*, rev. edn. (Albany, NY:
     State University of New York
     Press, 1993).
12 Nasr, *Islamic Science*, p.237.
13 Ibid, p.31.
14 Ibid, p.237.
15 Ibid, p.236.

CHAPTER EIGHT

1   White, O. F. and Mc Swain, C. J.,
     in *Beyond Methods: Strategies for
     Social Research*, ed. Gareth
     Morgan (Beverley Hills, CA: Sage
     Publications, 1983), p.297.
2   Williams, D., 'When is Naturalistic
     Evaluation Appropriate?,' *New
     Directions for Program
     Evaluation*, no. 30 (June 1986).
3   Ferguson, Marilyn, *The Aquarian
     Conspiracy: Personal and Social*

Transformation in the 80's (New York: J. P. Tarcher, Inc., 1987), p.163.

4 Ibid, p.163, 164.

5 Ibid, p.164.

6 Ibid.

7 Ibid, p.72.

8 Guba & Lincoln, *Naturalistic Inquiry*, p.37.

9 Ferguson, *Aquarian Conspiracy*, p. 394.

10 Zohar, Danah, *The Quantum Self* (New York: William Marrow & Co., Inc., 1990), p.72.

11 Bullington, J. & Karlson, G., 'Introduction to Phenomeno- logical Psychological Research,' *Scandinavian Journal of Psychology* (1984), p. 51.

12 Langeveld, 'Reflections on Phenomenology and Pedagogy,' *Phenomenology and Pedagogy*, vol.1, no.1 (1983).

13 al-Fārūqī, *Social and Natural Sciences*.

14 Ibid, p.11.

15 Ibid, p. 12.

16 al-Fārūqī, *The Cultural Atlas of Islam*, p. xii.

17 Chelkowski, Peter J., (ed.), *The Scholar and the Saint: Studies in Commemoration of Abu'l- Rayhan al-Bīrūnī and Jalal al-Din al-Rumi* (New York: New York University Press, 1975).

18 Ibid, p.75.

19 For more information on al- Bīrūnī's exploration of Hindu philosophy, see: Chelkowski, op.cit.

20 Sardar, *The Revenge of Athena*, p. 94.

21 Moustakas, Clark, *Heuristic Research: Design, Methodology and Applications* (Newbury Park, CA: Sage Publications, 1990).

22 Ibid, pp. 9, 11.

23 Ibid, p. 140.

24 Ibid, pp. 15-25.

25 Ibid, pp.27-34.

26 Morgan, G., *Beyond Methods*, pp. 295, 296.

27 Ibid, p.298.

28 Tesch, *Qualitative Research*, p.68.

29 Ibid, p.37.

30 Brown, Richard Harvey, *Society as Text: Essays on Rhetoric, Reason, and Reality* (Chicago, IL: University of Chicago Press, 1987).

31 Ricouer, P., *The Philosophy of Paul Ricouer* (Boston: Beacon, 1978), p.160.

32 Al-Fārūqī, I. R., *Al Tawḥīd: Its Implications for Thought and Life* (Herndon, Virginia: International Institute of Islamic Thought, 2000), p. 86.

33 Anastoos, C., 'A Comparative Survey of Human Science Psychologies,' in *Methods* (1987), p. 15.

34 Heshusius, Lous and Ballard, Keith (eds.), *From Positivism to Interpretivism and Beyond: Tales of Transformation in Educational and Social Research* (New York: Teachers College Press, 1996), p. 158.

35 Interested readers may refer to the

following authors on narrative as an inquiry: F. Connelly & D. Clandinin, *Teachers as Curriculum Planners* (New York: Teachers College of Columbia University, 1988); J. Mezirow, *Fostering Critical Reflection in Adulthood* (San Francisco: Jossey-Bass Publishers, 1990); and D. Thomas, *Flexible Learning Strategies in Higher and Further Education* (London: Cassell, 1995).

36 This is an extract from a correspondence between the author and Dr. D. Furlong. See note 2, ch.2).

CHAPTER NINE

1 Riegel, K., 'Toward a Dialectical Theory of Development,' *Human Development*, vol. 18, nos. 1, 2 (1975); *Psychology of Development and History* (New York: Plenum Press, 1976); and 'The Dialectics of Human Development,' *American Psychologist*, vol.31, no.9 (1976).

2 Basseches, Michael, *Dialectical Thinking and Adult Development* (Norwood, NJ: Ablex Pub. Corp., 1984).

3 Fowler, James W., *Faith: The Structural Development Perspective* (Cambridge, MA: Harvard University Press, 1975).

4 Basseches, *Dialectical Thinking*, p.9.

5 Ibid, p.21.

6 Ibid.

7 Ibid, p. 22.

8 Ibid.

9 Riegel, 'The Dialectics of Human Development,' p. 61.

10 Riegel, 'Toward a Dialectical Theory of Development.'

11 Fowler, *The Structural Development Perspective*, and *Stages of Faith: The Psychology of Human Development and the Quest for Meaning* (San Francisco, CA: Harper & Row, 1981).

12 Broughton, J., 'Genetics Metaphysics: The Developmental Psychology of Mind-Body Concepts,' *Body and Mind*, ed. R. Rieber (New York: Academic Press, 1980).

13 Riegel, 'Toward a Dialectical Theory of Development.'

14 Basseches, *Dialectical Thinking*.

15 Fowler, *The Structural Development Perspective*.

16 Ibid, p. 196.

17 Fowler, *Stages of Faith*, p.196.

18 Shah, Idries, 'Evolution' in *Reflections*, 2nd edn. (Baltimore, MD:Penguin Books, 1971), p.73.

19 Fowler, *Structural Development Perspective*, p.200.

20 Frobel, Friedlich, *The Education of Man*. Translated from the German by W. N. Hailmann (Clifton, NJ: A. M. Kelley, 1967), p.49.

21 Schimmel, Annemarie, *Mystical Dimensions of Islam* (Chapel Hill, NC: University of North Carolina Press, 1975), p. 219.

22 Ashraf, Syed Ali, 'The Inner Meaning of the Islamic Rites:

Prayer, Pilgrimage, Fasting, Jihad,'
in *Islamic Spirituality:*
Foundations, ed. Seyyed Hossein
Nasr, vol. 19 of *World Spirituality:*
An Encyclopedic History of the
Religious Quest (New York:
Crossroad, 1987), p.144.

23 Nasr, S., *World Spirituality*,
p.314.

24 Morgan, *Beyond Methods*.

25 Prigogine, Ilya, *From Being to*
Becoming: Time and Complexity
in the Physical Sciences (San
Francisco: Freeman, 1980).

26 Cited in Mahdi, 'The New
Wisdom,' p.30.

APPENDIX

1 Al Zeera, Z., 'The Collapse of
Westernised Universities in Islamic
Societies: Part 1: The Problem,'
unpublished Paper (University of
Toronto, 1988), p.2.

2 Guba, Egon and Lincoln, Yvonna
S., *Effective Evaluation*.

3 Guba and Lincoln, *Naturalistic*
Inquiry.

4 Simons, Helen, *Getting to Know*
Schools in a Democracy.

5 Covering letter for thesis proposal,
August 25, 1988.

6 Steiner, Rudolph, *The Roots of*
Education: Five Lectures Given in
Berne April 13th to 17th, 1924.
Translated by Helen Fox (London:
Rudolf Steiner P., 1968). Quoted
in *The Essential Steiner: Basic*
Writings of Rudolf Steiner, ed.
Robert A. Mc Dermott (San
Francisco, CA: Harper & Row,
1984), p.314.

7 Covering letter for the report dated
February 13, 1989 after Phase 1 of
the data collection completed.

8 Schutz, A. and Luckmann, T., *The*
Structures of the Life-World
(Evaston, IL: Northwestern
University Press, 1973), p.4.

9 Al Zeera, Z., 'The Collapse of
Westernized Universities in Islamic
Societies: Part 2. Reconciliation,'
paper presented at the VIIth World
Congress of Comparative
Education (Montreal, 1989), p.4.

10 Steele, R., *Freud and Jung,*
Conflicts of Interpretations (New
York: Harper and Row, 1982), p.
3.

11 Riegel, 'Toward a Dialectical
Theory of Development,' p.51.

12 Basseches, *Dialectical Thinking*
and Adult Development, p.58.

13 Steele, op.cit.

14 Al Zeera, Z., term paper for course
1360S, (1986).

15 A French politician, poet and
dramatist. Born 25th June, 1913 at
Basse-Point, Martinique.

BIBLIOGRAPHY

Abdul Haleem, M., 'The Hereafter and Here-and-Now in the Qur'an,' *The Islamic Quarterly*, vol.33, no.2 (1989).

Abul Quasem, Muhammad, *The Ethics of al-Ghazali: A Composite Ethics in Islam* (Petaling Jaya: Quasem, 1975).

Ahmad, Basharat, *The Qur'anic View of Human Freedom* (Lahore: Ahmadiyyah Anjuman Isha'at-i-Islam, 1969).

Ahmad, Khurshid, *Principles of Islamic Education*, 2nd edn. (Lahore: Islamic Publications, 1962).

Ahmad, Rais and Ahmad, Syed Naseem, eds., *Quest for New Science: Selected Papers of a Seminar* (Aligarh, India: Centre for Studies on Science, India International Printing Press, 1984).

Alatas, Hussein, *The Democracy of Islam: A Concise Exposition with Comparative Reference to Western Political Thought* (The Hague & Bandung: W. van Hoeve, 1956.

Alavi, S. M. Ziauddin, *Muslim Educational Thought in the Middle Ages* (New Delhi: Atlantic Publishers & Distributors, 1988).

Ali, Ahmed, *A Contemporary Translation of the Quran* (Princeton, NJ: Princeton University Press (1984).

Ali, Maulana Muhammad, *Arabic Text, English Translation and Commentary of the Holy Quran* (Chicago, Illinois: Specialty Promotions Co., Inc., 1973)

Ali, S. A., 'Islam and Modern Education,' *Muslim Education Quarterly*, vol. 4, no.3 (1982).

Ammarah, M., 'Arab Ummah: Does It have a Distinct Civilization Project?' *Akhbar Al-Khaleej* (January 7, 1990).

Anastoos, C., 'A Comparative Survey of Human Science Psychologies,' in *Methods* (1987), p.15.

Ansari, A.H., 'Transformation of the Perspective,' in *Aims and Objectives of Islamic Education,* ed. Syed Muhammad al-Naquib al-Attas (Sevenoaks, UK: Hodder & Stoughton; Jeddah: King Abdulaziz University, 1979).

Apple, M., *Ideology and Curriculum* (New York: Routledge, 1990).

Ashraf, Syed Ali, 'The Inner Meaning of the Islamic Rites: Prayer, Pilgrimage, Fasting, Jihad,' in *Islamic Spirituality: Foundations,* ed. Seyyed Hossein Nasr, vol. 19 of *World Spirituality: an Encyclopedic History of the Religious Quest* (New York: Crossroad, 1987).

—— 'Islamic vis-à-vis the Secularist Approaches,' *Muslim Education Quarterly*, vol. 4, no. 2 (1987).

al-Attas, Syed Muhammad al-Naquib, ed., *Aims and Objectives of Islamic Education* (Sevenoaks, UK: Hodder & Stoughton; Jeddah: King Abdulaziz University, 1979).

al-Azmeh, Aziz, *Arabic Thought and Islamic Societies* (London: Croom Helm, 1986).

Banaie, M. & Haque, N., *From Facts to Values: Certainty, Order, Balance and their Universal Implications* (Toronto, Canada: Optagon Publication, 1995).

Barazangi, Nimat Hafez, 'Arab Muslim Identity Transmission: Parents and Youth,' *Arab Studies Quarterly*, vol. 11, nos. 2 & 3 (1989).

Basseches, Michael, *Dialectical Thinking and Adult Development* (Norwood, NJ: Ablex Pub. Corp., 1984).

Bastick, Tony, *Intuition, How We Think and Act* (Chichester, UK; New York: John Wiley & Sons, 1982).

BaYunus, I., (1981). 'Education in Islamic society,' in *Education and Society in the Muslim World*, ed. M.W. Khan (Jeddah: King Abdul Aziz University).

Behishti, Muhammad Hosayni and Bahonar, Javad Bahonar, comps., *Philosophy of Islam*. Translated by M.A. Ansari (Accra: Islamic Seminary, 1982).

Berg, B., *Qualitative Research Methods for the Social Sciences* (Boston: Allyn and Bacon, 1989).

Bernstein, Richard J., *The Restructuring of Social and Political Theory* (New York: Harcourt Brace Jovanovich, 1976).

——*Beyond Objectivism and Relativism: Science, Hermeneutics, and Praxis* (Philadelphia, PA: University of Pennsylvania Press, 1983).

Biklen, S. and Bogdan, R., 'On Your Own with Naturalistic Evaluation,' *New Directions for Program Evaluation*, no. 30 (1986).

Bilgrami, H.H. and Ashraf, S.A.,*The Concept of an Islamic University* (London: Hodder & Stoughton; Cambridge, UK: Islamic Academy, 1985).

Bin Sayeed, Khalid, 'Islamic Resurgence and Societal Change,' *Islamic Culture*, vol. 60, no.1 (1986).

Bligh, Donald, ed., *Teach Thinking by Discussion* (Guildford, England, UK: Society for Research into Higher Education & NFER-Nelson, 1986).

Boisard, Marcel A., *Humanism in Islam* (Indianapolis, IN: American Trust Publications, 1988).

Brewer, Marilynn B. and Collins, Barry E., eds., *Scientific Inquiry and the Social Sciences: A Volume in Honor of Donald T. Campbell* (San Francisco, CA: Jossey-Bass, 1981).

Bronfenbrenner, V., 'Toward an Experimental Ecology of Human Development,' *American Psychologist*, vol. 32, no. 7 (1977).

Broughton, J., 'Genetics Metaphysics: The Developmental Psychology of Mind-Body Concepts,' in *Body and Mind*, ed. R. Rieber (New York: Academic Press, 1980).

Brown, Richard Harvey, *Society as Text: Essays on Rhetoric, Reason, and Reality* (Chicago, IL: University of Chicago Press, 1987).

Bowers, C. A., *The Promise of Theory: Education and the Politics of Cultural Change* (New York: Longman, 1984).

Bullington, J. & Karlson, G., 'Introduction to Phenomenological Psychological Research,' *Scandinavian Journal of Psychology* (1984).

Burgess, Robert G., ed., *Strategies of Educational Research: Qualitative Methods* (London; Philadelphia, PA: Falmer Press, 1985).

Chelkowski, Peter J., ed., *The Scholar and the Saint: Studies in Commemoration of Abu al-Rayhān al-Bīrūnī and Jalāl al-Dīn al-Rūmī* (New York: New York University Press, 1975).

Chisholm, Roderick M., ed., *Realism and the Background of Phenomenology* (Glencoe, IL: Free Press, 1960).

Chittick, W., 'Microcosm, Macrocosm and Perfect Man in the View of Ibn Al-Arabi,' *Islamic Culture*, vol. 63, nos. 1, 2 (1989).

Chomsky, Noam, *Problems of Knowledge and Freedom* (New York: Vantage Books, 1972).

Clark, Burton R., ed., *Perspectives on Higher Education: Eight Disciplinary and Comparative Views* (Berkeley, CA: University of California Press, 1984).

Connelly, F. & Clandinin, D., *Teachers as Curriculum Planners* (New York: Teachers College of Columbia University, 1988).

Daoudi, Mahmoud, 'An Introduction to the Implications of Human Nature for Ibn Khaldun's Thinking,' *The Islamic Quarterly*, vol. 32, no. 1 (1988).

Daud, Wan Mohd Nor Wan, *The Concept of Knowledge in Islam and Its Implications for Education in a Developing Country* (London; New York: Mansell, 1989).

De Bono, E., 'Critical Thinking Is not Enough,' *Educational Leadership*, vol. 42, no. 1 (1984).

——*I am Right, You are Wrong: From This to the New Renaissance, from Rock Logic to Water Logic* (London: Viking, 1990).

Denzin, N. K., 'The Logic of Naturalistic Inquiry,' *Social Forces*, vol. 50 (1971).

——*The Handbook of Qualitative Research* (Thousand Oaks, CA: Sage Publications, 1994).

Deutscher, I., 'Words and Deeds: Social Science and Social Policy,' in *Qualitative Methodology*, ed. W. Filstead (Chicago, IL: Markham, 1970).

Dewey, John, *Experience and Education* (New York: Collier Books, 1938).

——*Democracy and Education: An Introduction to the Philosophy of Education* (New York: Macmillan, 1961).

Dodge, Bayard, *Al-Azhar: A Millennium of Muslim Learning*, memorial edn. (Washington D.C: Middle East Institute, 1961).

——*Muslim Education in Medieval Times* (Washington D.C. : Middle East Institute, 1962).

Eaton, C. G., 'Man,' in *Islamic Spirituality: Foundations*, ed. Seyyed Hossein Nasr, vol. 19 of *World Spirituality: An Encyclopedic History of the Religious Quest* (New York: Crossroad, 1987).

Eisner, E., 'Educational Connoisseurship and Criticism,' in *Qualitative Approaches to Evaluation*, ed. David Fetterman (New York: Praeger, 1976).

——*The Educational Imagination* (New York: Macmillan Publishing Company, 1985).

Eisner, Elliot W. and Peshkin, Alan, eds., 'Qualitative Inquiry in Education: The Continuing Debate' (New York: Teachers College, Columbia University, 1990).

Ennis, R., 'A Logical Basis for Measuring Critical Thinking,' *Educational Leadership*, vol. 43, no. 2 (1985).

Farah, Talal Toufic, *Protection and Politics in Bahrain, 1869–1915* (Beirut: American University of Beirut, 1985).

Al-Fārūqī, Ismaʿīl R., 'Islamizing the Social Sciences,' *Studies in Islam*, vol. 16 (1979). Quoted in *Social and Natural Sciences: The Islamic Perspective*, ed. Ismaʿīl R. al-Fārūqī and Abdullah Omar Nasseef (Jeddah: Hodder & Stoughton, King Abdulaziz University, 1981).

——*Al Tawḥīd: Its Implications for Thought and Life* (Herndon, Virginia: International Institute of Islamic Thought, 2000).

Al-Fārūqī, Ismaʿīl R. and Lois Lamya,' *The Cultural Atlas of Islam* (New York: Macmillan, 1986).

Al-Fārūqī, Ismaʿīl R. and Nasseef, Abdullah Omar, eds., *Social and Natural Sciences: The Islamic Perspective* (Jeddah: Hodder & Stoughton, King Abdulaziz University, 1981).

Ferguson, Marilyn, *The Aquarium Conspiracy: Personal and Social Transformation in the 80's* (New York: J.P. Tarcher, Inc., 1987).

Fisk, D. W., *Scientific Inquiry and Social Sciences* (Jossey-Bass, Inc., 1981).

Foucault, Michel, *Language, Counter-memory, Practice: Selected Essays and Interviews*, ed. Donald F. Bouchard. Translated from the French by Donald F. Bouchard and Sherry Simon (Ithaca, NY: Cornell University Press, 1977).

Fowler, James W., *Stages of Faith: The Psychology of Human Development and the Quest for Meaning* (San Francisco, CA: Harper & Row, 1981).

——*Faith: The Structural Development Perspective* (Cambridge, MA: Harvard University Press, 1975).

Freire, Paulo, *Pedagogy of the Oppressed*. Translated by Myra Bergman Ramos (New York: Continuum, 1970).

——*Education for Critical Consciousness* (New York: Continuum, 1987).

Fröbel, Friedrich, *The Education of Man*. Translated from the German by W. N. Hailmann (Clifton, NJ: A. M. Kelley, 1987).

Gadamer, Hans-Georg, *Truth and Method* (New York: Crossroad, 1986).

Ghazzali, *The Alchemy of Happiness*. Translated from the Hindustani by Claud Field (London: Octagon, 1980).

Al-Ghazālī, *Mizān al-ʿAmal* (Cairo: Dār al-Maʿarif, 1964).

Geertz, Clifford, *The Interpretation of Cultures: Selected Essays* (New York: Basic Books, 1973).

Gibran, Kahlil, *The Garden of the Prophet* (New York: A. A. Knopf, 1933).

Glaser, Barney G. and Strauss, Anselm L., *The Discovery of Grounded Theory: Strategies for Qualitative Research* (Chicago, IL: Aldine Pub. Co., 1967).

Godwin, Joscelyn, *Robert Fludd: Hermetic Philosopher and Surveyor of Two Worlds* (London: Thames & Hudson, 1979).

Goldmann, Lucien, *The Hidden God: A Study of Tragic Vision in the Pensées of Pascal and the Tragedies of Racine*. Translated from the French by Philip Thody (London: Routledge & Kegan Paul; New York: Humanities Press, 1964).

Guba, E., 'Naturalistic Evaluation,' *New Directions for Program Evaluation*, no.34 (Summer, 1987).

——*The Paradigm Dialog* (Newbury Park, CA: Sage Publications, 1990).

Guba, Egon G. and Lincoln, Yvonna S., *Effective Evaluation* (San Francisco, CA: Jossey-Bass Publishers, 1981).

——*Naturalistic Inquiry* (Beverly Hills, CA: Sage Publications, 1985).

Habermas, Jürgen, *The Theory of Communicative Action*. Translated by Thomas McCarthy (Boston, MA: Beacon Press, 1984).

Hare, William, *Open-Mindedness and Education* (Montreal, Canada: McGill-Queen's University Press, 1979).

Heshusius, Lous and Balard, Keith, eds. *From Positivism to Interpretivism and Beyond: Tales of Transformation in Educational and Social Research* (New York: Teachers College Press, 1996).

Hjartland, L., 'Statistics as Fragmentors of Knowledge,' paper presented at a meeting of the International Conference for Social Philosophy on

Fragmentation of Knowledge, Capri, Italy, June, 1989.

Holloway, I., *Basic Concepts for Qualitative Research* (Malden, MA: Blackwell Science, 1997).

House, E., 'Justice in evaluation,' in *Evaluation Studies Review Annual*, ed. Gene V. Glass (Beverly Hills, CA: Sage Publications, 1976).

Hunt, David E., *Beginning with Ourselves: In Practice, Theory, and Human Affairs* (Cambridge, MA: Brookline Books; Toronto, Canada: OISE Press, 1987).

Husain, Syed Sajjad and Ashraf, Syed Ali, *Crisis in Muslim Education* (Sevenoaks, England, UK: Hodder & Stoughton; Jeddah: King Abdulaziz University, 1979).

Ikin, Graham, *Wholeness is Living: Scientific Thinking and Religious Experience* (London: Bles, 1970).

Iqbal, Muhammad, *The Reconstruction of Religious Thought in Islam* (Lahore: Javid Iqbal, 1968).

Kelly, E.F., 'Curriculum Evaluation and Literary Criticism,' in *Curriculum Theory Network* 5 (1975).

Kesarcodi-Watson, Ian, *Eastern Spirituality: Godhood of Man: Essays* (Delhi: Agam Prakashan; New Delhi: distributed by D. K. Publishers' Distributors, 1976).

Khan, Mohammad Wasiullah, ed., *Education and Society in the Muslim World* (Sevenoaks, England, UK: Hodder & Stoughton; Jeddah: King Abdulaziz University, 1981).

King, K., 'Two Key Fragmentations: That between Experimental Science and Social Science and that between Western and Third World Social Science.' Paper presented at a meeting of the International Institute for Social Philosophy on Fragmentation of Knowledge, Capri, Italy, June 18–23, 1989.

Kirk, J., *Reliability and Validity in Qualitative Research* (Beverley Hills: Sage Publications, 1986).

Kohlberg, L. and Mayer, R., 'Development as Aim of Education,' *Harvard Educational Review*, vol. 42, no. 4 (1979).

Kuhn, Thomas S., *The Structure of Scientific Revolutions* (Chicago, IL: University of Chicago Press, 1962).

Krikorian, Yervant H., ed., *Naturalism and the Human Spirit* (New York: Columbia University Press, 1944).

Krishnamurti, J., *Education and the Significance of Life* (New York: Harper, 1953).

——*Krishnamurti on Education* (New Delhi: Orient Longman, 1974).

——*The Wholeness of Life* (London: Victor Gollancz, 1978).

Langeveld, M., 'Reflections on phenomenology and pedagogy,' *Phenomenology and Pedagogy*, vol.1, no.1 (1983).

Lecompt, M., *The Handbook of Qualitative Research in Education* (San Diego, CA: Academic Press Inc., 1993).

Lemkow, Anna F., *The Wholeness Principle: Dynamics of Unity Within Science, Religion & Society* (London: Quest Books, 1990).

Lilley, Irene M., *Friedrich Froebel: A Selection from His Writings* (Cambridge, England, UK: Cambridge University Press, 1967).

Langgulung, Hassan, 'Ibn Sina as an Educationist,' *The Islamic Quarterly*, vol.32, no. 2. (1988).

Lincoln, Y. & Guba, E., 'But is it Rigorous? Trustworthiness and Authenticity in Naturalistic Evaluation,' *New Directions for Program Evaluation*, no.30 (June 1986).

MacDonald, B., 'Briefing Decision Makers,' *School Evaluation: The Politics and Process*, ed. E.R. House (Berkeley, CA: McCutchan, 1973)

—— 'Evaluation and Control of Education' in *SAFARI 1: Innovation, Evaluation, Research and the Problem of Control* (Norwich Center for Applied Research in Education, University of East Anglia, 1974)

—— 'The Experience of Innovation' in *CARE Occasional Publications no.6* (Center for Applied Research in Education, University of East Anglia, 1978a).

MacDonald, B. and Walker, R., 'Case Study and the Social Philosophy of Educational Research,' *Cambridge Journal of Education*, vol. 5, no.1 (1975).

Mahdi, M., 'The New Wisdom: Synthesis of Philosophy and Mysticism,' *The Encyclopedia Britannica*, vol. 22 (1987).

Mahesh, Maharishi, *The Science of Being and Art of Living* (New Delhi; New York: Allied Publishers, 1963.

Makdisi, George, *The Rise of Colleges: Institutions of Learning in Islam and the West* (Edinburgh: Edinburgh University Press, 1981).

Marcuse, Herbert, *One Dimensional Man: Studies in the Ideology of Advanced Industrial Society* (Boston, MA: Beacon Press, 1964).

Maritain, Jacques, *Education at the Crossroads* (New Haven, CT: Yale University Press; London: H. Milford, Oxford University Press, 1943). Quoted in *The Philosophical Foundations of Education*, comp. Steven M. Cahn (New York: Harper & Row, 1970).

Maspero, H., *Taoism and Chinese Religion* (Amerhurst: University of Massachusetts Press, 1981).

May, Rollo, *The Courage to Create* (New York: Norton, 1975). Quoted in Mordecai Richler, André Fortier, and Rollo May, *Creativity and the University* (Toronto, Canada: York University, 1975).

McMillan, J., 'Enhancing College Students' Critical Thinking: A Review of Studies,' *Research in Higher Education*, vol. 26, issue 1 (1987).

Melzer, John H., *An Examination of Critical Monism* (Ashland, OH: The University Post, 1937).

Messadi, Mahmoud, 'Cultural Development in the Arab States,' *Cultural Development: Some Regional Experiences* (Paris: UNESCO Press, 1981).

Mezirow, J., *Fostering Critical Reflection in Adulthood* (San Francisco: Jossey-Bass Publishers, 1990).

Miller, John P., *The Holistic Curriculum*, Toronto, Canada: OISE Press, Ontario Institute for Studies in Education, 1988).

Misra, Ganeswar, *Sources of Monism: Bradley and Sankara* (Meerut, India: Anu Books, 1986).

Mol, Hans, *Wholeness and Breakdown: A Model for the Interpretation of Nature and Society* (Madras: Dr. S. Radhakrishnan Institute for Advanced Study in Philosophy, University of Madras, 1978).

Morgan, Gareth, ed., *Beyond Method: Strategies for Social Research* (Beverly Hills, CA: Sage Publications, 1983).

Moustakas, Clark, *Heuristic Research: Design, Methodology, and Applications* (Newbury Park, CA: Sage Publications, 1990).

Murata, S., 'Masculine–Feminine Complementary in the Spiritual Psychology of

Islam, *The Islamic Quarterly*, vol. 33, no.3 (1989).

Mutahhari, M., *Foundations of Islamic Thought* (Berkeley, CA: Mizan Press, 1985).

Naqvi, Syed Nawab Haider, *Ethics and Economics: An Islamic Synthesis* (Leicester, UK: Islamic Foundation, 1981).

Nasr, Seyyed Hossein, *Islamic Science: An Illustrated Study* (London: World of Islam Festival Pub. Co., 1976).

——(ed.), *Islamic Spirituality: Foundations*, vol. 19 of *World Spirituality: An Encyclopedic History of the Religious Quest* (New York: Crossroad, 1987).

——'The Qur'an as the Foundation of Islamic Spirituality,' in *Islamic Spirituality: Foundations*, ed. Seyyed Hossein Nasr, vol. 19 of *World Spirituality: An Encyclopedic History of the Religious Quest* (New York: Crossroad, 1987).

——'The Cosmos and the Natural Order,' in *Islamic Spirituality: Foundations*, ed. Seyyed Hossein Nasr, vol. 19 of *World Spirituality: An Encyclopedic History of the Religious Quest* (New York: Crossroad, 1987).

——*Knowledge and the Sacred* (Albany, NY: State University of New York Press, 1989).

——*An Introduction to Islamic Cosmological Doctrines: Conceptions of Nature and Methods Used for Its Study by the Ikhwān al-Safa', al-Bīrūnī, and Ibn Sina*, rev. edn. (Albany, NY: State University of New York Press, 1993).

——*The Need for a Sacred Science* (Albany, NY: State University of New York Press, 1993).

Nasr, Seyyed Hossein and Leaman, Oliver, eds., *History of Islamic Philosophy* (London; New York: Routledge, 1996).

Netton, Ian Richard, *Allah Transcendent: Studies in the Structure and Semiotics of Islamic Philosophy, Theology, and Cosmology* (London; New York: Routledge, 1989).

Noddings, Nel, *Caring: A Feminine Approach to Ethics & Moral Education* (Berkeley, CA: University of California Press, 1984).

Noddings, Nel and Shore, Paul J., *Awakening the Inner Eye: Intuition in Education* (New York: Teachers College, Columbia University, 1984).

Oakeshott, Michael Joseph, *Experience and Its Modes* (Cambridge, England,

UK: The University Press, 1933).

——*Rationalism in Politics, and Other Essays* (London: Methuen, 1962).

——*The Voice of Liberal Learning: Michael Oakeshott on Education*, ed. Timothy Fuller (New Haven, CT: Yale University Press, 1989).

Parlett, M. & Hamilton, D., 'Evaluation as Illumination,' in *Occasional Paper 9* (Center for Research in the Educational Sciences, University of Edinburgh, 1972).

Patton, Michael Quinn, *Qualitative Evaluation Methods* (Beverly Hills, CA: Sage Publications, 1980).

Paul, R. W., 'Critical Thinking: Fundamental to Education for a Free Society,' *Educational Leadership*, vol. 42, no.1 (1984).

Pellegrini, A.D., *Narrative Thought and Narrative Language*, eds. Bruce Britton and A.D. Pellegrini (Hillsdale, N.J.: Lawrence Erlbam Associates, 1990)

Polanyi, Michael, *Personal Knowledge: Towards a Post-Critical Philosophy* (Chicago, IL: University of Chicago Press, 1958).

——*Beyond Nihilism* (Cambridge: University Press, 1960).

——*The Tacit Dimension*, Anchor Books edn.(Garden City, NY: Anchor Books, 1967).

——*Scientific Thought and Social Reality: Essays*, ed. Fred Schwartz (New York: International Universities Press, 1974).

Popper, Karl R., *Conjectures and Refutations: The Growth of Scientific Knowledge* (New York: Harper & Row, 1968).

Prigogine, Ilya, *From Being to Becoming: Time and Complexity in the Physical Sciences* San Francisco: Freeman, 1980).

Quraishi, Mansoor A., *Some Aspects of Muslim Education* (Baroda [Vadodara], Gujarat, India: Centre of Advanced Study in Education, Faculty of Education and Psychology, M.S. University of Baroda, 1970).

Radhakrishnan, Sarvepalli and others, eds., *History of Philosophy: Eastern and Western* (London: Allen & Unwin, 1953).

Rahman, Fazlur, *The Philosophy of Mulla Sadra* (Albany, NY: State University of New York Press, 1975).

——*Islam & Modernity: Transformation of an Intellectual Tradition*

(Chicago, IL: University of Chicago Press, 1982).

Raskin, Marcus G., 'Ending the Faustian Bargain,' in *New Ways of Knowing: The Sciences, Society, and Reconstructive Knowledge,* by Marcus G. Raskin and others (Totowa, NJ: Rowman & Littlefield, 1987).

Ricouer, P., *The Philosophy of Paul Ricouer* (Boston: Beacon, 1978).

Riegel, K., 'Dialectic Operations: The Final Period of Cognitive Development,' *Human Development*, vol. 16, no.5 (1973).

——'Toward a Dialectical Theory of Development,' *Human Development*, vol. 18, nos. 1, 2 (1975).

——*Psychology of Development and History* (New York: Plenum Press, 1976).

——'The Dialectics of Human Development,' *American Psychologist*, vol. 31, no.9 (1976).

Riegel, Klaus F. and Meacham, John A., eds., *The Developing Individual in a Changing World* (The Hague, The Netherlands: Mouton, 1976).

Rippey, R. (ed.), *Studies in Transactional Evaluation* (Berkeley, CA: McCutchan, 1973).

Rudhyar, Dane, *Rhythm of Wholeness* (Wheaton, IL: Theosophical Pub. House, 1983).

Sabetti, Stephano, *The Wholeness Principle* (Sherman Oaks, CA: Life Energy Media, 1986).

Said, Hakim Mohammad and Khan, Ansar Zahid, *al-Bīrūnī: His Times, Life and Works* (Karachi: Hamdard Academy, 1981).

El Sakkakini, Widad, *First Among Sufis: The Life and Thought of Rabia al-Adawiyya, the Woman Saint of Basra.* Translated by Nabil Safwat (London: Octagon Press, 1982).

Saqib, Ghulam Nabi, *Modernization of Muslim Education in Egypt, Pakistan, and Turkey: A Comparative Study* (Lahore: Islamic Book Service, 1983).

Sardar, Ziauddin, ed., *The Revenge of Athena: Science, Exploitation, and the Third World* (London: Mansell, 1988).

Schimmel, Annemarie, *Mystical Dimensions of Islam* (Chapel Hill, NC: University of North Carolina Press, 1975).

Schuon, Frithjof, *Understanding Islam*. Translated by D.M. Matheson (London: Allen & Unwin, 1963).

——*The Transcendent Unity of Religions*. Translated by Peter Townsend (New York: Pantheon, 1953).

Scriven, M., 'Objectivity and Subjectivity in Social Research,' in *Philosophical Redirection for Social Research*, ed. L.G. Thomas (Chicago: University of Chicago Press, 1972).

Shah, Idries, *The Sufis* (Garden City, NY: Doubleday, 1964).

——'Evolution,' in *Reflections*, by Idries Shah, 2nd edn. (Baltimore, MD: Penguin Books, 1971).

——'Evolution,' in *Reflections by Idries Shah*, 2nd edn. (Baltimore, M.D.: Penguin Books, 1971).

Sharif, M. M., ed., *A History of Muslim Philosophy: With Short Accounts of Other Disciplines and the Modern Renaissance in Muslim Lands* (Wiesbaden, Germany: Harrassowitz, 1963).

Sherif, Mohamed Ahmed, *Ghazali's Theory of Virtue* (Albany, NY: State University of New York Press, 1975).

Sherman, Robert R. and Webb, Rodman B., eds., *Qualitative Research in Education: Focus and Methods* (New York: Falmer Press, 1988).

Siddiqui, M. N., 'Restructuring the Study of Economics in Muslim Universities,' in *Social and Natural Sciences: The Islamic Perspective*, ed. Isma'il. R al-Fārūqī and Abdullah Omar Nasseef (Jeddah: King Abdulaziz University, 1981).

Simons, Helen, *Getting to Know Schools in a Democracy: The Politics and Process of Evaluation* (London; New York: Falmer Press, 1987).

Stake, R., *Evaluating the Arts in Education* (Colombus, O.H.: Charles E. Merrill Publishing Company, 1975).

Steiner, Rudolf, *The Philosophy of Spiritual Activity: Fundamentals of a Modern View of the World. Results of Introspective Observations According to the Method of Natural Science*. Translated from the German by Rita Stebbing; ed. Paul M. Allen (West Nyack, NY: Rudolf Steiner Publications, 1963).

——*Truth and Knowledge: Introduction to 'Philosophy of Spiritual Activity.'* Translated from the German by Rita Stebbing; ed. Paul M. Allen, 2nd edn.

(Blauvelt, NY: Steinerbooks, 1981).

——*The Roots of Education: Five Lectures Given in Berne April 13th to 17th, 1924*. Translated by Helen Fox (London: Rudolf Steiner P., 1968). Quoted in *The Essential Steiner: Basic Writings of Rudolf Steiner*, ed. Robert A. McDermott (San Francisco, CA: Harper & Row, 1984).

Al-Tajir, Mahdi Abdalla, *Bahrain, 1920–1945: Britain, the Shaikh, and the Administration* (London; New York: Croom Helm, c.1987).

Tarthang, Tulku. *Love of Knowledge* (Berkeley, CA: Dharma Pub., 1987).

Taylor, Steven J. and Robert Bogdan, *Introduction to Qualitative Research Methods: The Search for Meanings*, 2nd edn. (New York: John Wiley, 1984).

Tesch, Renata, *Qualitative Research: Analysis Types and Software Tools* (New York: Falmer Press, 1990).

Thomas, D. (ed.), *Flexible Learning Strategies in Higher and Further Education* (London: Cassell, 1995).

Tibawi, A. L., *Islamic Education: Its Traditions and Modernization into the Arab National Systems* (London: Luzac, 1972).

El Tom, B., 'Education and Society,' in *Education and Society in the Muslim World*, ed. Mohammad Wasiullah Khan (Sevenoaks, England, UK: Hodder & Stoughton; Jeddah: King Abdulaziz University, 1981).

Totah, Khalil A., *The Contribution of the Arabs to Education* (New York: Teachers College, Columbia University, 1926).

Umaruddin, M., *The Ethical Philosophy of al-Ghazzali* (Aligarh, India: Muslim University, 1962).

Vahiduddin, S., 'The Qur'anic Vision of God, Man and His Destiny,' *Islamic Culture*, vol.60, no.1 (1986).

Wax, Rosalie H., *Doing Fieldwork: Warnings and Advice* (Chicago, IL: University of Chicago Press, 1971).

White, O.F. and McSwain, C.J., in *Beyond Method: Strategies for Social Research*, ed. Gareth Morgan (Beverly Hills, CA: Sage Publications, 1983).

Wightman, W., *Science and Monism* (London: Allen, 1934).

Williams, D., 'When is Naturalistic Evaluation Appropriate,' *New Directions for Program Evaluation*, no. 30 (June 1986).

Wing, R. L., *The Tao of Power* (Garden City, NY: Doubleday, 1986).

Wolf, R., 'The Use of Judicial Evaluation Methods in the Formation of Educational Policy,' in *Educational Evaluation and Policy Analysis, 1* (May-June, 1974).

Young, Michael F. D., ed., *Knowledge and Control: New Directions for the Sociology of Education* (London: Collier-Macmillan, 1971).

Young, R. and Collin, A., 'Career Development and Hermeneutical Inquiry. Part I: The Framework of a Hermeneutical Approach,' *Canadian Journal of Counseling*, vol. 22, no. 3 (1988).

Al Zeera, Z., 'An ESP Program as a Communicative Approach to Language Teaching in the College of Health Sciences in Bahrain,' MA thesis (UWIST, Cardiff, Wales, UK: 1981).

——'Evaluation of the Orientation Program at the University of Bahrain: A Socio-cultural Perspective,' PhD thesis (University of Toronto, Canada: 1990).

Zohar, Danah, *The Quantum Self* (New York: William Marrow & Co., Inc., 1990).

GENERAL INDEX